# THE JEWELER'S ART

by Katherine Nell Macfarlane

**LUCENT BOOKS**

*An imprint of Thomson Gale, a part of The Thomson Corporation*

Detroit • New York • San Francisco • New Haven, Conn. • Waterville, Maine • London

To Lisa Yount
for her kind support and encouragement
this book is affectionately dedicated

© 2007 Thomson Gale, a part of The Thomson Corporation.

Thomson and Star Logo are trademarks and Gale and Lucent Books are registered trademarks used herein under license.

*For more information, contact*
Lucent Books
27500 Drake Rd.
Farmington Hills, MI 48331-3535
Or you can visit our Internet site at http://www.gale.com

| LIBRARY OF CONGRESS CATALOGING-IN-PUBLICATION DATA |
| --- |
| Macfarlane, Katherine Nell.<br>  The jeweler's art / by Katherine Nell Macfarlane.<br>    p. cm. — (Eye on art)<br>  Includes bibliographical references and index.<br>  ISBN 978-1-59018-984-9 (hardcover)<br>  1.  Jewelry—History.  I. Title.<br>NK7306.M33 2007<br>739.2709—dc22<br>                                                                    2007007804 |

ISBN-10:1-59018-984-1
Printed in the United States of America

# CONTENTS

Foreword. . . . . . . . . . . . . . . . . . . . . . . . . . . . . . . . . . . 5
Introduction . . . . . . . . . . . . . . . . . . . . . . . . . . . . . . . . 8
    Jewelry Through the Ages

Chapter One. . . . . . . . . . . . . . . . . . . . . . . . . . . . . . . 10
    Ancient Times (to 500 B.C.)

Chapter Two. . . . . . . . . . . . . . . . . . . . . . . . . . . . . . . 21
    The Greeks and the Romans (500 B.C. to A.D. 500)

Chapter Three . . . . . . . . . . . . . . . . . . . . . . . . . . . . . 32
    The Early Middle Ages (A.D. 500 to 1000)

Chapter Four . . . . . . . . . . . . . . . . . . . . . . . . . . . . . . 44
    The Romanesque and Gothic Eras (A.D. 1000 to 1450)

Chapter Five. . . . . . . . . . . . . . . . . . . . . . . . . . . . . . . 54
    The Renaissance (A.D. 1450 to 1600)

Chapter Six. . . . . . . . . . . . . . . . . . . . . . . . . . . . . . . . 63
    Baroque and Rococo (A.D. 1600 to 1815)

Chapter Seven . . . . . . . . . . . . . . . . . . . . . . . . . . . . . 76
    The Victorians and Edwardians (A.D. 1815 to 1915)

Chapter Eight. . . . . . . . . . . . . . . . . . . . . . . . . . . . . . 89
    The Modern Jeweler's Art

Notes . . . . . . . . . . . . . . . . . . . . . . . . . . . . . . . . . . . . 101
Glossary . . . . . . . . . . . . . . . . . . . . . . . . . . . . . . . . . . 104
For Further Reading. . . . . . . . . . . . . . . . . . . . . . . . . . 106
Index. . . . . . . . . . . . . . . . . . . . . . . . . . . . . . . . . . . . . 108
Picture Credits . . . . . . . . . . . . . . . . . . . . . . . . . . . . . 111
About the Author. . . . . . . . . . . . . . . . . . . . . . . . . . . 112

# Foreword

*"Art has no other purpose than to brush aside . . . everything that veils reality from us in order to bring us face to face with reality itself."*
—French philosopher Henri-Louis Bergson

Some thirty-one thousand years ago, early humans painted strikingly sophisticated images of horses, bison, rhinoceroses, bears, and other animals on the walls of a cave in southern France. The meaning of these elaborate pictures is unknown, although some experts speculate that they held ceremonial significance. Regardless of their intended purpose, the Chauvet-Pont-d'Arc cave paintings represent some of the first known expressions of the artistic impulse.

From the Paleolithic era to the present day, human beings have continued to create works of visual art. Artists have developed painting, drawing, sculpture, engraving, and many other techniques to produce visual representations of landscapes, the human form, religious and historical events, and countless other subjects. The artistic impulse also finds expression in glass, jewelry, and new forms inspired by new technology. Indeed, judging by humanity's prolific artistic output throughout history, one must conclude that the compulsion to produce art is an inherent aspect of being human, and the results are among humanity's greatest cultural achievements: masterpieces such as the architectural marvels of ancient Greece, Michelangelo's perfectly rendered statue *David*, Vincent van Gogh's visionary painting *Starry Night*, and endless other treasures.

The creative impulse serves many purposes for society. At its most basic level, art is a form of entertainment or the means for a satisfying or pleasant aesthetic experience. But art's true power lies not in its potential to entertain and delight but in its ability to enlighten, to reveal the truth, and by doing so to uplift the human spirit and transform the human race.

One of the primary functions of art has been to serve religion. For most of Western history, for example, artists were paid by the church to produce works with religious themes and subjects. Art was thus a tool to help human beings transcend mundane, secular reality and achieve spiritual enlightenment. One of the best-known, and largest-scale, examples of Christian religious art is the Sistine Chapel in the Vatican in Rome. In 1508 Pope Julius II commissioned Italian Renaissance artist Michelangelo to paint the chapel's vaulted ceiling, an area of 640 square yards (535 sq. m). Michelangelo spent four years on scaffolding, his neck craned, creating a panoramic fresco of some three hundred human figures. His paintings depict Old Testament prophets and heroes, sibyls of Greek mythology, and nine scenes from the Book of Genesis, including the Creation of Adam, the Fall of Adam and Eve from the Garden of Eden, and the Flood. The ceiling of the Sistine Chapel is considered one of the greatest works of Western art and has inspired the awe of countless Christian pilgrims and other religious seekers. As eighteenth-century German poet and author Johann Wolfgang von Goethe wrote, "Until you have seen this Sistine Chapel, you can have no adequate conception of what man is capable of."

In addition to inspiring religious fervor, art can serve as a force for social change. Artists are among the visionaries of any culture. As such, they often perceive injustice and wrongdoing and confront others by reflecting what they see in their work. One classic example of art as social commentary was created in May 1937, during the brutal Spanish civil war. On May 1 Spanish artist Pablo Picasso learned of the recent attack on the small Basque village of Guernica by German airplanes allied with fascist forces led by Francisco Franco. The German pilots had used the village for target practice, a three-hour bombing that killed sixteen hundred civilians. Picasso, living in Paris, channeled his outrage over the massacre into his painting *Guernica*, a black, white, and gray mural that depicts dismembered animals and fractured human figures whose faces are contorted in agonized expressions. Initially, critics and the public condemned the painting as an incoherent hodgepodge, but the work soon came to be seen as a powerful antiwar statement and remains an iconic symbol of the violence and terror that dominated world events during the remainder of the twentieth century.

The impulse to create art—whether painting animals with crude pigments on a cave wall, sculpting a human form from marble, or commemorating human tragedy in a mural—thus serves many purposes. It offers an entertaining diversion, nourishes the imagination and the spirit, decorates and beautifies the world, and chronicles the age. But underlying all these functions is the desire to reveal that which is obscure—to illuminate, clarify, and perhaps ennoble. As Picasso himself stated, "The purpose of art is washing the dust of daily life off our souls."

The Eye on Art series is intended to assist readers in understanding the various roles of art in society. Each volume offers an in-depth exploration of a major artistic movement, medium, figure, or profession. All books in the series are beautifully illustrated with full-color photographs and diagrams. Riveting narrative, clear technical explanation, informative sidebars, fully documented quotes, a bibliography, and a thorough index all provide excellent starting points for research and discussion. With these features, the Eye on Art series is a useful introduction to the world of art—a world that can offer both insight and inspiration.

# Introduction

## Jewelry Through the Ages

Self-adornment is a basic human instinct. The most primitive people decorate their bodies with paint, feathers, flowers, and shells, weave and embroider their clothing in colorful patterns, and sew ornaments onto it.

When human technology advanced to shaping metals and colorful stones, jewelry made from these materials became a favored form of adornment because it was both beautiful and durable. It was also regarded as something of value because it required rare materials and special skills to make. In addition, it became a mark of prestige, with complex political, religious, and magical significance. The jewels of the Egyptian pharaohs were not mere personal adornments; they were the insignia of a god on earth, just as the brilliant regalia of the Byzantine emperors marked them as God's earthly viceroy. Medieval Christians kissed their bishop's ring as a sign of reverence, and lords and ladies wore golden reliquaries set with precious stones in the hope of divine protection. So powerful was the fascination of jewels that precious stones themselves acquired magical properties for good or ill. Until the 1800s it was not unusual for laws to be handed down governing which ranks in society could wear what sorts of jewelry.

Wearing jewelry for personal adornment and pleasure was a relatively late development. The Greeks were the first society known to make precious ornaments a privilege of the common man (and woman) as well as of the ruler and priest, and if the discoveries at Pompeii and Herculaneum are any indication, the Romans followed suit. This democratic attitude was revived in the Renaissance and became widespread from the 1800s onward. Pieces of jewelry came to have great personal and sentimental meaning for those who wore them. Today, wearing jewelry is everyone's right and everyone's pleasure, and jewelry is a beautiful and valuable means of expressing one's individual tastes and personality.

During the Renaissance, women freely adorned their bodies, and even their hair, with jewelry.

# Ancient Times (to 500 B.C.)

Treasures uncovered by archaeologists can tell a great deal about the jewelry-making techniques of ancient peoples. They show what kind of metals they worked and how they worked them. They show whether they worked precious and semiprecious stones, and which ones. They show whether their stonework was crude or elegantly finished and whether their use of the stones was simple or elaborate. Sometimes they even reveal what sort of tools the jewelers used. It is fortunate for archaeologists that two ancient civilizations, the Sumerians and the Egyptians, were firm believers in taking the comforts and pleasures of this life, including abundant jewelry, into the next one. Sumerians and Egyptians were buried wearing the jewelry they treasured in life. It is also fortunate that in at least the two cases of Queen Puabi of Ur and King Tutankhamen of Egypt, archaeologists uncovered tombs undisturbed and unlooted by the tomb robbers of ancient and modern times.

## Dressed to Die: The Treasure of Queen Puabi

Queen Puabi was laid to rest in the so-called Royal Tombs of Ur sometime during the Third Dynasty of Ur (2112 to 2004 B.C.).

Ur was one of several city-states that made up Sumer, an ancient civilization in Mesopotamia, the land between the Tigris and Euphrates rivers in what is now Iraq. Sir Charles Leonard Woolley, at the head of an expedition sponsored by the British Museum and the University of Pennsylvania, excavated the city of Ur, including its royal tombs, between 1922 and 1934. He had the great good fortune to uncover the queen's unrifled tomb and its extraordinary riches.

## Sumerian Jewelry Making

The treasures found in Ur's royal tombs show that even as early as 2000 B.C., the Sumerians knew how to render gold and other metals, including silver, and had mastered certain basic metal-working skills. To judge from archaeological finds, Sumerian metal crafters preferred working in gold rather than silver. They probably did so not because they considered gold more precious than silver but because gold occurs naturally in pure form, either

Examples of Sumerian stone and beadwork, using gold, lapiz lazuli, carnelian, and silver.

in veins (lodes) or in deposits as nuggets and gold dust in rivers and streams, whereas silver has to be refined (freed from mineral compounds by a process of melting the ore). Gold is also softer than silver and therefore is easier to work.

Two qualities of gold make it especially suitable for simple metalworking: It is malleable (it can be hammered into thin sheets with nothing more complicated than a heavy mallet on a flat, solid work surface), and it is ductile (it can be drawn or rolled into slender wires). Sumerian goldsmiths made great use of both sheet gold and gold wire.

Once gold is hammered into a thin sheet, it can be put to various uses. The simplest is to cut it into long strips or ribbons. Sheet gold can also be cut into more complex shapes (leaves, flowers, animals), which can then be engraved by using one of two techniques: chasing, in which details are pressed into the metal from the front with a sharp stylus; or repoussé, in which the metal is pressed or hammered from behind either against a soft material (wax or leather) or into a mold, or die, to form a larger, raised detail on the front. Sheet gold can also be hammered over a wooden core to form either a hollow object or a metal casing for the core. Large and elaborate items were made in several pieces and soldered together, using an alloy that melted at a lower temperature than the gold. Gold, silver, and electrum (an alloy of gold and silver) were also hammered into small three-dimensional sculptures.

One of the most spectacular examples of Sumerian sheet-gold working is the Golden Helmet of Mescalamdug, which Woolley discovered in the simple grave of that great prince. As Woolley describes it,

> It was a helmet of beaten gold made to fit low over the head with cheek pieces to protect the face, and it was in the form of a wig, the locks of hair hammered up in relief, the individual hairs shown by delicate engraved lines. Parted down the middle, the hair covers the head in flat wavy tresses and is bound round with a twisted fillet; behind it is tied into a little chignon, and below

the fillet hangs in rows of formal curls about the ears, which are rendered in high relief and are pierced so as not to interfere with hearing; similar curls on the cheek pieces represent whiskers; round the edge of the metal are small holes for the laces which secured inside it a padded cap, of which some traces yet remained.[1]

The helmet as a whole was most likely hammered into, or over, a mold. It was probably made in several pieces, which were then soldered together. The details of the hair and fillet were added by chasing.

Besides being masterful metalworkers, the Sumerians were skilled at stonecutting, stone carving, and bead drilling, using lapis lazuli, carnelian, and various kinds of agate. While lapis lazuli, a dark blue stone often starred with specks of iron pyrite, is fairly soft (which may account for its popularity with Sumerian jewelry makers), red-orange carnelian and agate, which are forms of quartz, are quite hard and more difficult to work. It is not known what sorts of tools the Sumerians used for bead making, but they were probably similar to those found in Egypt during the same period: polishing wheels and drilling tools of flint and perhaps copper.

The Sumerians also excelled at inlay work, in which small pieces of stone or other materials are glued into a recessed background, rather like mosaic. Complex inlays, done in shell, lapis lazuli, red stone, and sometimes gold and silver, can be seen on the Great Lyre of Ur and the so-called Standard of Ur. Neither is a piece of jewelry (one is a musical instrument, the other a hollow wooden box whose real purpose is unknown), though they are masterpieces of the inlayer's art. Sumerian inlay artists apparently had discovered neither the cements used by later artisans nor the ability to make metal settings for the inlay work. Inlay was held in place with bitumen (tar).

# Queen Puabi's Diadem

Queen Puabi's diadem, or ornamental crown, was a masterpiece of the Sumerian jeweler's art. To quote Woolley, the diadem consists of "a broad gold ribbon festooned in loops round the hair . . . ; over this came three wreaths, the lowest hanging down over the forehead, of plain gold ring pendants, the second of beech leaves, the third of long willow leaves in sets of three with gold flowers whose petals were of blue and white inlay; all these were strung on triple chains of lapis and carnelian beads."[2]

The willow leaves of the topmost wreath are cut from sheet gold, with red-orange carnelian beads suspended from their tips. Between the leaf clusters are threaded lapis lazuli beads and repoussé gold rosettes, their petals inlaid alternately with lapis lazuli and a white, enamel-like material.

The sheet-gold beech leaves of the second wreath are delicately engraved to show their veins and also tipped with car-

## QUEEN PUABI

The queen was a small woman, just under 5 feet (1.5m) tall. She was no longer young, perhaps even elderly by the standards of her people, in her late thirties or early forties. She outlived her lord and husband—Charles Leonard Woolley notes that the king's burial was disturbed to accommodate hers. A cylinder seal found beside her body identifies her as "Puabi, the Queen."

She was laid to rest as befit a great queen. In addition to her diadem, she was adorned in a shimmering cape of beads: gold and polished agate, carnelian, and lapis lazuli. She wore a ring on every finger, three bead necklaces of semiprecious stones, and a belt fashioned of gold, carnelian, and lapis lazuli beads. She was buried with her household around her: five guards with bronze daggers, four teamsters to drive her ox-drawn funeral sledge, her master of the wardrobe, and ten handmaidens in golden jewels and headdresses, bearing musical instruments to entertain their lady in the hereafter.

nelian beads. Between the leaves are spacers of long cylindrical lapis beads and small flat carnelian beads. The fringe of gold hoops is suspended from a band of lapis lazuli and carnelian beads. On either side, below the wreaths and the gold hoops, the gold ribbon is draped in three graceful loops on either side, framing the queen's face and hair.

Puabi's hair was secured in back with what Woolley described as a golden Spanish comb, from which spring seven stems. Each stem ends in a six-petaled, golden repoussé flower, the center of which is inlaid with lapis lazuli. The Queen's head ornaments are completed with a pair of large golden double-crescent-moon earrings.

The Sumerian techniques of jewelry making as well as the materials were spread by caravans carrying rich stones and metals throughout the Middle East. The Egyptians learned a great deal from the Sumerians about working gold and silver and precious stones, and what they learned they added to, to an extraordinary degree.

This ornamental crown of a Sumerian lady of the court, discovered during the excavations at Ur, is very similar in nature to Queen Puabi's diadem.

## A Boy-King's Regalia: The Tomb of Tutankhamen

Tutankhamen, pharaoh from 1332 to 1322 B.C., came to the throne as a child and did not reign long enough to make much of an impact on history. Perhaps because of his insignificance, his tomb lay undisturbed until 1922, when an archaeologist and Egyptologist named Howard Carter, excavating in the Valley of the Kings, discovered it. Carter and his sponsor, George Herbert, known as Lord Carnarvon, partially opened the doorway into the tomb and peered in. As Carter described the experience,

At first I could see nothing, the hot air escaping from the chamber causing the candle to flicker, but presently, as my eyes grew accustomed to the light, details of the room within emerged slowly from the mist, strange animals, statues, and gold—everywhere the glint of gold . . . when Lord Carnarvon . . . inquired anxiously "can you see anything?" it was all I could do to get out the words "Yes, wonderful things."[3]

These "wonderful things" that Carter and Lord Carnarvon had discovered were among the finest and most beautiful examples of Egyptian jewelry making.

# Egyptian Jewelry Making

Archaeological discoveries show that even as early as the beginning of the dynastic period, around 3000 B.C., the Egyptians were skilled metalworkers. They had mastered the art of making sheet gold and gold foil, and they made gold wire that they used in various ways, including winding it into a spiral to make lozenge-shaped beads. They also made beads by pressing sheet gold into a hemispherical mold, then soldering the two halves into a hollow round bead. A bracelet found in the tomb of Djer, who ruled sometime between 3000 and 2750 B.C., has beads of this sort. Another bracelet from Djer's tomb, as described by Hans Wolfgang Müller and Eberhard Thiem in *Gold of the Pharaohs*, has a rosette "in the shape of the pistil of a lotus flower . . . a masterpiece of early goldsmiths' work. . . . The outer corona . . . of the rosette would have been made by pressing the gold into a die."[4] Such molds could even be made from natural objects. A necklace found at Nag ed-Deir is made of gold spiral shells that "may have been produced by taking a plaster impression from a real shell and pressing the gold foil into the hollow forma."[5]

Even at this early time the Egyptians understood the process of casting, in which molten metal is poured into a mold. A third bracelet from Djer's burial is made of alternating plaques of gold and turquoise. "The regular shape of each gold falcon

Much of the beadwork and inlay in Egyptian jewelry were made of a material called faience. Faience, as used by the Egyptians, is a ceramic made almost entirely of ground quartz. Colorants of various sorts were added either directly to the quartz paste or in a glaze. When the object was fired, it emerged with a dazzling color: blue green, carnelian red, soft yellow, cobalt blue, or violet. Faience was also used to make small ceramic objects, such as the Metropolitan Museum's beloved mascot, William the Hippopotamus.

indicates that they are casts,"[6] according to Müller and Thiem. To create these flat, one-sided plaques, the goldsmiths probably used a simple method of casting in which they poured molten gold into a form that was either stamped into a soft substance like sand, or made of a substance like fired clay that could be used over and over. Later, objects done in the round (three-dimensional), such as small statuary and elements attached to larger metalworks, were cast using the lost wax method: A model of the object was made in wax, then covered in ceramic material and fired, causing the wax to melt and run out of the mold. Then molten gold was poured into the hollow mold; when it had cooled and hardened, the mold was removed.

The Egyptians were also skilled at the kind of enamelwork known as cloisonné, in which fine wire is soldered to a metal background to form the outline of a design. Enamel "paste" of various colors is then applied in the spaces outlined by the wire, and the object is fired to bond the enamel to the metal.

From the earliest period, the Egyptians were skilled bead makers. Müller and Thiem remark on the large numbers of

**O**f course there were rumors of foul play. The deceased was only nineteen years old, and a king and a god besides. He went to his grave with a crushed chest and a broken leg. Of course, he might have been killed in battle; a pharaoh was expected to fight alongside his troops. Or it may have been a simple case of a "car" accident—driving too fast, as teenagers will, in a light chariot like the ones found in his tomb. However he died, he was given a royal farewell. He took with him, besides his chariots and armchairs and gameboards and model boats and linen underwear and packets of roast duck, an incredible hoard of jewelry, the finest of the jeweler's art for his time. When Howard Carter and his crew opened Tutankhamen's innermost solid gold coffin, they found the king's head and shoulders covered by a magnificent burial mask, also of solid gold and decorated with exquisite inlay work.

beads of semiprecious stone such as lapis lazuli, purple amethyst, turquoise, and carnelian that were shaped, carved, polished, and drilled: "Their manufacture presupposes the existence of specialized workshops in the settlements of the Nile Valley."[7] The remains of a bead factory from around 2000 B.C. proves that bead makers could achieve impressive effects using relatively simple flint and bronze tools. The Egyptians excelled particularly at weaving tube-shaped beads of semiprecious stone, glass, and faience (a ceramic material) into the characteristic wide "collar" necklace so typical of Egyptian adornment.

The Egyptians were also masters of stonecutting and polishing. Tutankhamen's treasure contains many examples of beautifully cut and polished cabochons (convex, unfaceted gems) which were set into jewelry with a bezel, a metal strip surrounding the stone. They also produced beautiful carved gems, such as scarab beetles (a symbol of the sun and eternal life), that were set into jewelry.

Most of all, the Egyptians excelled at inlay work. In the earlier technique, the goldsmith used a chisel to gouge out a channel that fit the inlays precisely, and the cut stone was then cemented into place. Inlayers used semiprecious stone, glass, or faience. Later, channels were made by soldering narrow wires or strips of metal to a background to form a raised pattern, into which the inlay was cemented. Many beautiful examples of inlay work were found in Tutankhamen's tomb. One of the loveliest is a winged scarab pectoral (pendant worn on the chest). The scarab itself is carved from lapis lazuli; it is supporting a sun disk of carnelian, and its wings are inlaid with glass and semiprecious stones.

## Tutankhamen's Burial Mask

The mask that covered the face and shoulders of Tutankhamen's mummy captures the imagination of all who see it. The twenty-two-pound mask was hammered out of heavy sheet gold, although individual elements, such as the vulture and serpent

King Tutankhamen's burial mask is inlaid with semiprecious stones, faience, and glass.

goddesses on the royal headband, were cast, probably by the lost wax method. The mask is an idealized portrait of the young king, exquisitely modeled and inlaid with semiprecious stones, faience, and glass.

The royal headcloth and Tutankhamen's ceremonial false beard are inlaid with blue glass. The vulture goddess on the headband has a beak of glass, and the cobra goddess's head is made of blue faience. The cobra's body is inlaid with lapis lazuli, carnelian, quartz, and turquoise glass. The king's wide collar is inlaid with semiprecious stones carved to resemble the tube beads used in wide necklaces: deep blue lapis lazuli, red quartz, and green feldspar. It is edged with an ornamental row of cloisonné enamel lotus-bud drops.

The Mesopotamians and Egyptians had perfected the basic metalworking and stoneworking techniques of jewelry making. The richness and formal quality of the jewelry, however, indicates that it was the adornment of great nobles and god-kings. The goldsmith's skills would be refined and perfected over the next thousand years, as jewelry became less the prerogative of royalty and more the adornment of everyday life.

# The Greeks and
# the Romans
# (500 B.C. to A.D. 500)

The Greeks and the Romans mark the beginning of truly historical times. A good deal of both written and pictorial information exists about their taste in jewelry, which is fortunate because relatively little physical evidence exists aside from valuables that were buried in out-of-the-way places like southern Russia, or jewels that were buried where looters and amateur archaeologists could not get at them, as in the Roman cities buried by the eruption of Mount Vesuvius. Anything easy to lay hands on was carried off by invading barbarians, broken up or melted down for its precious metals and stones, remade into jewelry of later times, or casually destroyed.

## Greek and Roman Jewelry Making

The Greeks were the master jewelry makers of antiquity. They refined the techniques discovered by earlier civilizations and created sophisticated and delicate jewelry that would not look out of place in a showcase at Tiffany's. To quote Elizabeth Stasinopoulos, an archaeologist with the National Archaeological Museum of Athens,

The Mesopotamians and the Egyptians had developed advanced metalworking techniques long before the Greeks, and so it is natural that the Greeks learned these from them. However, as in other forms of art so in metalworking, the craftsmen selected those elements they wanted and quickly adapted them to their own aesthetic perceptions, creating decorative themes that far outshone the commonplace repetitive designs of the artifacts of the East.[8]

The Romans borrowed liberally from the Greeks (and liberally borrowed Greek goldsmiths as well, marching them off into slavery or enticing them to Rome with the promise of wealthy clients). They contributed little to the tradition of classical jewelry making but a taste for pearls and colored stones, particularly carved intaglios and cameos, a trend that actually began among the Hellenistic Greeks.

## Greek Metalworking

Greek jewelry during the classical period (500 to 400 B.C.) tended to be modest and restrained. This may have been due to the Greeks' inherent good taste, but, as Guido Gregorietti remarks in *Jewelry Through the Ages*, it was "probably due to a shortage of gold." He adds, "During the Classical period, when sculpture achieved such heights, the minor arts, above all gold work and jewelry, developed little and were in any case restricted by the many finance laws which were passed at that time."[9]

During the Hellenistic period (after 400 B.C.), following the conquests of Alexander the Great, the Greeks had access to abundant sources of gold and precious stones. Influenced by the wealth and flamboyant tastes of Asia, they made generous use of the gold and began to explore the possibilities of the precious stones. Earrings, which in the classical period were modest buttons or florets, might now feature minute statues of Nike, goddess of victory, driving a two-horse chariot, or baskets of fruit and flowers with pendant acorns or pinecones. A diadem found at Kerch in southern Russia is adorned with a Herakles knot set with garnets, sea serpents, a winged Victory, and nine elaborate gold tassels decorated with florets and garnet beads.

One characteristic of Greek jewelry making in all periods was a fondness for nature motifs. Many designs were copied from plants, particularly flowers and leaves. The stylized palmetto leaf and lotus flower, so popular on Greek pottery, were also used in jewelry, as was the acanthus leaf. One very common style of necklace, sometimes referred to as the "acorn" necklace, consisted of a string of acorn-shaped pendants attached to beads or a chain; the pendants might also be shaped like stylized pinecones, lotus buds, leaves, or fruits. Animal motifs were also popular: lions, horses, bulls, rams, dolphins, birds, and bees. Serpentine bracelets were especially popular with both the Greeks and the Romans. The serpent in ancient times had no evil associations; sacred to Asclepius, it was thought to ward off illness and injury.

The Greeks surpassed earlier cultures in metalworking. Unlike the Mesopotamians and Egyptians, who made lavish use of semiprecious and precious stones, the Greeks concentrated on skillfully shaping and embellishing the metal itself. Stasinopoulos says of them, "Whereas for the Oriental peoples semi-precious stones were structural elements of their jewellery, in Greece emphasis was placed on modelled decoration. The jewellers used gold and silver . . . to fashion diadems, necklaces, bracelets, earrings and rings of unrivalled artistry."[10]

In several types of metalworking the Greeks particularly excelled: casting figures in the round; relief (figures raised above a flat background), both

Hellenistic jewelry that featured little statuettes, such as this pair of earrings, was common in the first century.

cast and repoussé; chain work and braiding gold wire into mesh; granulation; and cloisonné. They invented none of these techniques; all were known to some degree to the Egyptians. But the Greeks perfected them to an extraordinary degree.

The lost wax method of casting that the Greeks used for their bronze statuary they also applied, on a much smaller scale, to gold and silver jewelry. Little statuettes were incorporated into necklaces and earrings: pert sphinxes with enigmatic smiles, plump cupids, animals and monsters of all sorts, heads of goddesses and grotesques, little winged statues of the god Pan. As Stasinopoulos explains, where casting in pure gold was prohibitive, Greek jewelers would cast

> a core of silver or copper . . . to which very fine gold leaf was applied, affixed to the surface by simply rolling its edges or with the help of some adhesive. Another

The Greeks excelled in many types of metalworking, including chains both large and small. This painting illustrates a fine chain hairnet.

method, which required a smaller quantity of gold, was gilding with mercury. Gold and mercury form a semi-fluid amalgam with which the object was covered. Because mercury has a much lower boiling point than gold it evaporated on heating, leaving a fine film of gold on the surface of the object. Silvered jewellery usually had a copper core. Because the melting point of silver is much lower than that of copper, objects could be silvered by dipping them in molten silver. The method of coating with a mercury amalgam, described above, was also applied.[11]

The Greeks used repoussé from the beginning. By the classical period they had learned to cast intricate bronze dies for stamping sheet gold. Gold formed in this way was then soldered together in two halves to create in-the-round hollow beads and other complex elements, or used as raised, low-relief designs on flat surfaces. Such low-relief designs were often used in medallions holding delicate gold and jeweled women's hairnets. The Greeks also made regular use of stamping—hammering a patterned bronze punch into sheet gold against a soft surface such as leather or sand to make a repeated raised pattern.

Granulation is the technique of soldering tiny gold spheres or granules or gold dust (powder granulation) to a gold background to create designs, or an overall frosted effect as on the Silenus necklace from Ruvo. Although the Egyptians used granulation to some extent, it was perfected by the Greeks and Etruscans, after which it dwindled away and became a lost art. Gregorietti speculates that "the granules were probably made by placing pieces of gold . . . between layers of powdered charcoal in a crucible. When heated the pieces of gold melted into minute spheres separated from each other by the charcoal. The charcoal was then washed away, and the granules graded for size by passing them over a punched sheet till each slotted into a hole of its own diameter."[12]

The greater mystery is how the Greeks and Etruscans soldered these minute spheres to each other and to the gold background so that the soldering was not visible. The likeliest theory is that they used a copper compound mixed into a resin or glue that secured the granulation to the base, which was then heated; at the proper temperature the resin burned away, releasing the copper to alloy with the gold and form an on-the-spot solder.

The chains and gold mesh that the Greeks produced are very nearly as regular as those made by modern machines. A flat strip of chain work or braided gold wire was often the base for the popular "acorn" necklace and was also used in belts, bracelets, and diadems. Intricate chains attached dangles to earrings and connected ornaments on necklaces. Heavier chains or thick tubes of meshwork supported a single pendant or pectoral. Fine chains were even woven into hairnets.

## Greek Enamel Work

Like the Egyptians, the Greeks used cloisonné enamel work to add color to jewelry, and for the most part preferred it to colored stones, although they sometimes combined the two with dazzling effect, as in the exquisite coronet from the Tomb of Gold at Canosa. But they particularly favored patterns of gold wire as decorative elements in their own right, either soldered to a gold background or made into openwork designs, a technique known as filigree.

## Greek and Roman Stonework

The Romans, unlike the Greeks, adored colored stones and preferred them to enamel, little of which appears in Roman jewelry. They carried on earlier techniques of polishing beads and cabochons, although they favored a wider range of stones, including many we think of as precious. They particularly loved emeralds and pearls; Pliny the Elder saw Lollia Paulina, wife of Emperor Caligula, at a private dinner party "covered with emeralds and pearls interlaced alternately and shining all over her head, hair, ears, neck, and fingers."[13]

The Romans readily adopted the Hellenistic taste for carved stones. Intaglio, in which an image is carved in reverse into the

# THE ETRUSCANS

The Etruscans were a mysterious people—no one knows where they came from, and we have only glimmerings of their language, which resembled neither Greek nor Latin. They arrived in Italy, possibly from Asia Minor, sometime after 700 B.C. Most of what we know about them comes from their tombs, which honeycomb the hillsides of Umbria, north of Rome. They laid their dead away in carved and frescoed chambers pulsing with joyous energy—feasting and dancing, chariot racing, hunting and fishing.

The Etruscan zest for life is reflected in their jewelry. They followed the Greek fashion for the most part but added an element of their own exuberance. Necklaces have not one tier of ornaments but several, acorns and fruit and flowers, satyr heads and winged deities, even polished agates and amber in finely worked gold settings, all connected by an intricate web of chains. The Etruscans particularly loved granulation. Lavishly granulated lions, sphinxes, chimeras, and griffins march on parade on one golden fibula; fantastic creatures done in powder granulation adorn another. Etruscan ladies wore gold bracelets stamped with intricate repoussé work, elaborate earrings rich with granulation and filigree and dangles, and regal gold diadems. The effect must have been dazzling.

A sampling of gold Etruscan jewelry.

surface of the stone, was known to the Sumerians, who used it for cylinder seals; but the Greeks perfected its three-dimensional quality, creating elegantly naturalistic reverse reliefs for use in signet rings. Stone carving was considered an art form, and the names of some of the masters are known. Pliny the Elder mentions "an edict of Alexander the Great forbidding his likeness to be engraved . . . by anyone except Pyrgoteles, who was undoubtedly the most brilliant artist in this field. Next to him in fame have been Apollonides, Cronius and the man who made the excellent likeness of Augustus . . . which his successors have used as their seal, namely Dioscurides."[14]

The cameo, in which the image is carved in relief, was a Greek innovation.

The cameo, in which the image is carved in relief, was a Hellenistic innovation. Although it was common to carve cameos on single-color stones such as red jasper or chalcedony, the finest were made from banded stones such as onyx, carved

so that the lighter figure stood out against a dark background, as in the Gonzaga Cameo depicting Nero and his mother Agrippina.

Greek stone carvers produced their magnificent effects with very simple tools, such as sharpened quartz stones. Pliny notes that "there is a great difference between one stone and another in that some cannot be engraved with an iron tool and some only with a blunt iron tool, although all can be worked with a diamond point."[15]

Some of the finest examples of Roman jewels, and the most characteristic, have been found in the excavations of the resort city of Pompeii, buried in the eruption of Mt. Vesuvius in A.D. 79. The people who kept town houses at Pompeii were the well-to-do middle class, and

The Tovsta Mohyla pectoral was discovered in the kurgan, or burial mound, of a Scythian warrior in southern Ukraine. The Scythians were nomadic horsemen whom the Greeks associated with the Amazons. Scythian taste in jewelry inclined toward the massive and flamboyant, yet they had an eye for elegant workmanship, and goldsmiths in the Greek colonies along the Black Sea catered to their desires.

The spirit of the Tovsta Mohyla pectoral is Scythian, but the workmanship is Greek. The topmost of three tiers of figures, in the finest tradition of Greek naturalism, depicts high-relief vignettes of Scythian daily life: Two men in Scythian trousers stitch a sheepskin, mares and cows nurse their young, servants milk sheep. After a second tier featuring birds and blossoms, the third tier returns to naturalistic, high-relief figures. In three central groupings, a pair of griffins attack a horse. On one side of these, a lion and lioness bring down a stag; on the other a similar pair stalks a boar. Whoever cast the griffins certainly knew his griffins. Their bodies are lionlike down to the muscled haunches and whippy tails, their heads are perfect birds of prey, and every feather in their great wings is engraved with great detail.

their homes and their jewelry reflected, better than the lavish adornments of the imperial family, the tastes of average Romans.

# The Emerald Necklace from Pompeii

The young woman took refuge near the door in an interior room of the villa—perhaps planning her escape into the countryside, away from the pumice and ash raining down from Mount Vesuvius.

But instead, she was struck down by a surge of superheated volcanic gases, ash and rock fragments that brought death almost immediately. The woman was entombed with her most treasured possessions, among them a gold and emerald necklace, a hoard of coins and two gold bracelets shaped like snakes.[16]

The lady's necklace was perhaps not so grand as Empress Lollia Paulina's parure, but its design was tasteful and elegant. The base was a wide band of gold mesh onto which bezel-set rough-cut emeralds and cabochon-cut baroque pearls were alternately set. The choice of these large, irregular gems seems to have been intentional. As one admirer observes of the necklace, "Since the mesh and the clasp are obviously the work of a superb craftsman, the use of the stones with large simple shapes must have been deliberate and carefully thought out." The same author says of Pompeian jewelry and Roman jewelry generally,

A gold armband in the form of a snake, found in the excavations of Pompeii in A.D. 79.

# She Was Middle-Aged and Homely

They found her body on the waterfront. No place for a respectable lady of means, but sometimes even a respectable lady of means has to get out of town in a hurry. She had bundled up her jewelry and was down on the beach looking for a fast boat out of town when her killer caught up with her and snuffed out her life. The killer did not bother to rob the lady, had no interest in her fine gold rings set with green jasper and a ruby engraved with a strutting bird, her serpent bracelets with glittering jasper eyes, her delicate pearl earrings.

The lady died in a blast of superheated gas from the eruption of Mt. Vesuvius in A.D. 79. The rain of volcanic debris that followed buried the Roman seaside town of Herculaneum and the lady, who would not be found for more than nineteen hundred years. In one of the most poignant descriptions of the remains that she is reconstructing, physical anthropologist Sara Bisel says of the Ring Lady, "She was certainly homely, but someone cared enough to give her beautiful things."

Quoted in "After 2,000 Years of Silence, the Dead Do Tell Tales at Vesuvius," *National Geographic*, May 1984, p. 560.

"This taste for openwork and for light, abstract, bubbly forms characterizes much jewelry found at Pompeii and amounts to a fashion trend of Imperial times, away from the modeled, often representational elements of Greek jewelry."[17]

Unfortunately, the Romans' light-hearted and stylish approach to personal adornment came to an end as the Roman Empire collapsed under a failing economy and barbarian invasions from beyond its borders. Jewelry in the centuries to follow was massive, impressive, and purely functional.

# 3

# The Early Middle Ages (A.D. 500 to 1000)

The taste of the early Middle Ages was characterized by a move away from the restraint and refinement of classical Greece and Rome toward gaudy display. Nowhere was this tendency more evident than in early medieval jewelry. There was a corresponding move away from the private nature of Greek and Roman jewelry, of which the purpose was personal pleasure and adornment. In the centuries following the end of the Roman Empire, the function of jewelry was increasingly public, whether its purpose was to promote the image of imperial power and majesty, as in Byzantium, or, as in western Europe, to impress the population (and potential invaders) with the prowess and strength of the local war chief.

There was also a move away from the naturalism of classical art generally, toward greater stylization. This tendency seems to be typical of the art of people living in interesting but not particularly settled times. As life became more and more uncertain, art became more and more structured, as if people no longer felt comfortable with the physical world in which they found themselves.

# The Golden Age of the Byzantine Empire

The Roman Empire, which had been tottering for a couple of centuries, fell in A.D. 476, and what was left of it transferred its seat of power to the eastern Mediterranean and Constantinople. There it continued as the Byzantine Empire until 1453, when the city fell to the Ottoman Turks. The Byzantine Empire enjoyed a golden age, when it was the mightiest political power in the western world, from the fall of Rome to about A.D. 800; thereafter its power and its influence on western Europe steadily declined.

The fact that this eastern Roman Empire was Greek had little bearing in itself on the style of jewelry produced in the centuries following 476; jewelry manufacture in Greek and Roman times had always been predominantly Greek. What did affect the Byzantine jewelers' art, in addition to the styles of the Middle East, was an increased regimentation in the society as a

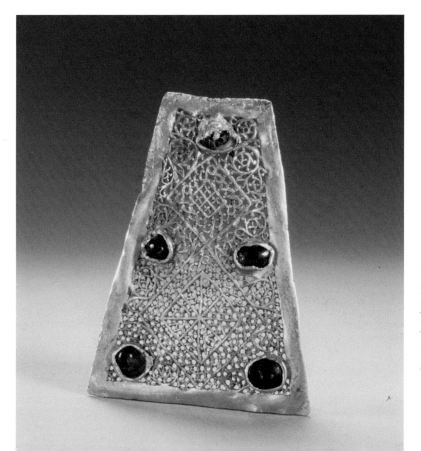

As seen by this piece of Byzantine jewelry, Byzantine jewelers favored abstract designs and geometric shapes.

A Byzantine cross pendant with the Virgin Mary flanked by Saints Basil the Great and Gregory Thaumaturge.

whole that is reflected in stiffness and stylization, as well as greater ostentation, in the jewelry produced.

## The Byzantine Jeweler's Art

Byzantine jewelers followed techniques they inherited from Greek goldsmiths in the classical and Hellenistic periods (repoussé and chasing, granulation, filigree, and enameling), with certain differences. The style of all types of jewelry was generally much simpler. Chains were still made, attractive, sometimes ingenious, but nowhere near as intricate as those made during the classical and Hellenistic periods. They were generally single chains rather than meshwork, made of comparatively large, heavy links.

Instead of human and animal forms, Byzantine jewelers favored abstract designs and geometric shapes. Where motifs were representational, they were less naturalistic, more formulaic. The jeweler's technique itself was often crude compared to the work of previous centuries, as if the craftsmen became less skillfully trained and their clients less refined and demanding. This decline in standards had been going on throughout the last two hundred years and may have been due to the rise of Christianity, which preached against earthly vanity (at least for private persons). It may also have been due to the "melting pot" quality of the late empire, in which Roman citizens from the barbarian hinterlands rose to positions of wealth and power.

Christian motifs and iconography (formalized representations of certain figures and symbols; for example, Christ, the Virgin, saints, and doves) were popular. Religious jewelry such as the *enkolpion*, a small reliquary (container for a relic, a bit of something belonging to a saint or martyr) worn as a pendant, and amulets of all sorts abounded. Even when an item of jewelry was not specifically religious in nature, crosses or other Christian symbols were often worked into its elements; for example, the openwork fastening rings of Byzantine necklaces.

Two techniques introduced in the Byzantine era appear to have come from the Middle East: niello and opus interassile. As Stasinopoulos explains, niello is a method of applying a black design to a metal background: "The design is first engraved on the surface of the object and the spaces are then filled with a pulverized mixture of sulphur compounds of silver, copper and

These Byzantine rings are examples of the niello technique, whereby a black design is applied to a metal background.

lead. Since this mixture has a lower melting point than the [back]ground metal, it melts on heating and fills the motifs, thus creating a lustrous black decoration on the surface of the objects." [18]

Opus interassile is an alternative to filigree for creating openwork jewelry. According to Stasinopoulos, "The decoration was first drawn on the metal and then selected parts were removed with different drills and saws, creating perforated designs reminiscent of lacework."[19]

As the demand for glitter and show replaced the demand for skilled metalwork, precious stones and pearls came to dominate jewelry design. Massed colored stones were used to create a multicolored effect. Where earlier stonecutters favored simple cabochons and expressed their ingenuity in intaglio and cameo pieces, the Byzantines had a taste for shaped and faceted stones. Earrings often have a central, stone-encrusted plaque from which cylindrical or faceted beads dangle. Necklaces consist of stones of complementary colors, connected by links of chain.

Byzantine earrings often featured a central, stone-encrusted plaque from which cylindrical or faceted beads dangled.

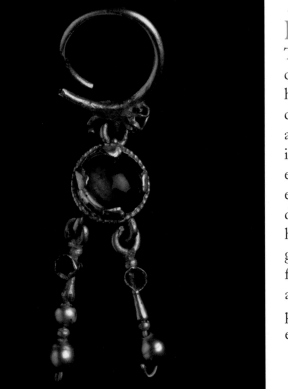

## The Jewels of Empress Theodora

Theodora's mosaic portrait in the church of San Vitale at Ravenna shows how she appeared on state occasions, as classicist Robert Browning says, "stiff and hieratic [ceremonial] in the glittering brocades and jewels of a Roman empress."[20] She literally drips with enormous pearls. They adorn her diadem, they are braided into her hair and hang down in long perpendula (dangling ornaments) on either side of her face. She wears an emerald necklace and earrings of emerald, pearl, and sapphire. Her breast and shoulders are covered by a massive pectoral decorated

with yet more pearls, two enormous rubies, and an emerald set into a rectangular plaque.

Theodora's finery is not merely for show. In combination with her formal, stylized pose and purple cloak they signify that she is earthly authority personified, static and unchanging. However,

> Theodora represents more than just herself as Empress. But what? The representation of the three Magi on the hem of her garment gives us a hint . . . it serves to make the allusive connection between the bringing of gifts (as she and Justinian are doing) and the Magi's gifts to Christ and the Virgin Mary at the Nativity. This connection establishes an analogy between Jesus-Mary and the Emperor-Empress.[21]

Theodora, with "her halo, magnificent crown, purple robe, and lavish jewels"[22] stands as the Virgin's representative on

Empress Theodora's (third from left) jewels represented the power and glory of the Byzantine Empire and the Christian Church.

# THE CIRCUS GIRL

**M**ost of what is known about Theodora comes from the historian Procopius. This would not have pleased Theodora, for Procopius was her bitter enemy. Procopius wrote that Theodora was the daughter of a circus bear trainer married to an actress, considered most unsavory professions at the time. According to Procopius, Theodora followed her mother onto the stage and also became a courtesan of a rather low order. She married the soldier who would become the Emperor Justinian in A.D. 527, and thereafter, in spite of her scandalous past, behaved with exemplary decorum. She proved to be an empress of courage, shrewdness, and astute political instincts. One of Justinian's retainers wrote that her intelligence was equal to any man's. In 532 she faced down a riotous mob to save her husband's throne, remarking, "I like the old saying, that the purple is the noblest shroud." She was always Justinian's most trusted counselor.

Quoted in Robert Browning, *Justinian and Theodora*. New York: Praeger, 1971, p. 112.

Earth, as Emporer Justinian, facing her across the sanctuary of the church, is Christ's.

Theodora's jewels emphasized the power and glory of the Byzantine Empire and the Christian Church. The grave goods of a Saxon king in southern England testify to another sort of power—prowess in battle and the ability to defend his land and people.

## An Anglian King's Ship Burial

In western Europe the centuries following the fall of Rome were a time of turmoil, and life was hard. Rome's armies had been withdrawn to defend Italy, and barbarian hordes in search of new lands and plunder poured across the undefended borders from the north and east. Beset as they were by migrations, invasions, and the general lawlessness that followed the collapse of the Roman Empire, people concentrated on the essentials in life.

# Jewelry Making in the Early Middle Ages

What we think of as jewelry proper—rings, earrings, and bracelets—are rare in western Europe during this period, perhaps because such things were expensive, nonessential, and an encumbrance to the active and sometimes desperate lives these people led.

Necklaces are found occasionally, either pendants connected by chain work on the Greco-Roman and Byzantine model, or solid, hinged models of one or more rings. Much more common are brooches, which were not only ornamental but functional, used to secure cloaks and other garments. To quote Alex Croom, curator of the Arbeia Roman Fort, "In many ways they should be viewed as part of the clothing itself, in the same way that buttons are today."[23] Of these, the fibula (an ornamental safety pin), which appeared in Greco-Roman times, continued to be popular, particularly the "crossbow" fibula, which Gregorietti describes as the "buckler variety with fan heads, arched bridges and a flat or moulded foot."[24] It appears to have been a military, or at least a male, fashion. Brooches were also round, S-shaped, or zoomorphic (shaped like birds or animals); eagles were particularly popular, such as a garnet-encrusted specimen found at Cesena, Italy. S-shaped brooches were often zoomorphic as well, with one or two animal heads, such as the two-headed dragonesque type. Women wore brooches in pairs, often but not always matching, to fasten their outer gown—a simple tube or even unsewn length of fabric—at the shoulders. The so-called turtle brooches, which often occur in matched pairs, were used for this purpose. Brooches worn this way were sometimes connected by a decorative necklace of metal links or beads. One particular style that emerged at this time was the penannular brooch, a circular brooch with a sliding metal pin that was pushed through the fabric and fastened by passing it through and resting it on the circle. Brooches are found alongside other decorative but functional elements of dress: buckles, strap ends, purse clasps and decorations, and fittings for armor made and adorned by the goldsmith.

Goldsmiths in western Europe throughout the period drew on both Roman and Byzantine forms and techniques. The jewelry of the Anglo-Saxons, a warlike Germanic people who overran England in the A.D. 400s, was often decorated with niello. Filigree, enameling, and colored stones were also popular as decoration for brooches, which were often covered so thickly that, as Gregorietti says, they had "the appearance of a miniature stained-glass window with gold supports instead of lead."[25] A

## THE PENANNULAR BROOCH

The penannular brooch evolved out of the annular, or ring, brooch, which consisted of a metal circle, through which the material to be fastened was pulled, and a sliding pin, onto which it was then fed. The tip of the pin rested on the top of the ring, and the weight of the cloth pulling on it kept it in place. Ring brooches were usually simple, often made out of bronze, but could be very rich and elaborate, as in the case of the Hunterston Brooch. A penannular brooch is almost a ring but has a gap in the circle to make pinning easier. The ring is flipped up, the shaft of the pin is stuck through the material, and then the pin is passed through the gap in the ring and the ring slid around under the pin to hold the material in place.

The origin of the penannular brooch was probably Celtic, although the Vikings also adopted it. Eventually it became so exaggerated that a law was passed in Scotland limiting the length of the pin. There is a Jellinge-style thistle-headed brooch in the British Museum with a pin over 20 inches (51.2cm) in length; in a pinch it could become a formidable weapon.

popular variation on red enamel was the use of thin slices of gar-net cut to shape and cemented into the metal cells.

Jewelry makers also adopted styles of the people they worked among and for, Celtic, Germanic, or Scandinavian. One type of decoration that became popular during the early Middle Ages was what is referred to generally as the Jellinge style (although Jellinge was one of half a dozen related styles). It is named for a town in Denmark where there are rune stones carved in this manner, but it probably was adapted from the intertwining Celtic knot designs such as appear in manuscripts of the period. Jeff Clarke, a reenactor and researcher of Viking clothing and jewelry, describes it as "restless" and "characterised by a seething mass of surface ornament, which is largely of stylised animals or more correctly zoomorphic designs."[26]

Brooches during the Byzantine era were often zoomorphic; that is, they were shaped like birds or animals.

The love of nature and the realistic depiction of its creatures is a characteristic of people who have tamed it. The lady who wears earrings with cute animal faces on them does not expect to encounter a wolf in her living room.

The people of the early Middle Ages knew all about nature and its creatures: Nature was powerful and the animals were fearsome, and the people did not want to decorate their jewelry with either. They preferred nice, abstract, and above all, orderly geometric shapes and carpet patterns. When they depicted animals at all, they did so in an extremely stylized, controlled manner. The figures become zoomorphic design elements rather than lifelike representations. Often it requires careful examination to pick out the animals at all. Yet even in this abstract form these animals are monsters, creatures out of a nightmare. They writhe across the surfaces they decorate, clawing and biting each other or gnawing their own tails.

The one exception to this unflattering view of animals is their use as royal emblems to represent courage and prowess in battle, like the wolves on the Sutton Hoo purse lid; though even here it is debatable whether the wolves are doing homage to the man between them or devouring him.

Several stunning examples of this type of decoration were found during the excavation of the Sutton Hoo ship burial in 1939.

## The Treasure of Sutton Hoo

Some time after A.D. 620, at Sutton Hoo on the bank of River Deben in southeastern England, an East Anglian king was laid to rest in his longboat with his regalia around him. His personal ornaments were typical of the elegant but extremely functional jewels of war displayed by western European nobles during the early Middle Ages. The great gold buckle that fastened his waist belt weighs nearly a pound, and is lavishly decorated in the Jellinge fashion with writhing beasts picked out in niello. In addition, he had a sword belt fastened with a buckle decorated with blue cloisonné and garnet inlay. It matches the hilt of his sword and the shoulder clasps that secured his leather armor. On all these, the gold beneath the garnet inlays is textured so that the pattern shows through the transparent stone, and the enameling is minutely detailed. The king also wore a large purse full of gold coins, attached with hinged straps to his waist belt, which may explain the need for the belt's massive buckle. The purse's lid, perhaps of whalebone ivory, was decorated with gold and cloisonné plaques in the Jellinge style.

Two of the plaques, which depict a pair of wolves bracketing a man, may give a clue to the king's identity: The design suggests that he was one of the Wulfingas, "sons of the wolf," a prominent Anglian tribe. Such a man was Raedwald, *bretwalda* (high king) of the East Angles, who died around A.D. 625.

In spite of, or perhaps because of, men like Raedwald, eventually the invasions and upheavals came to an end, and with the spread of Christianity, western Europe gradually settled into a time of comparative peace. From it grew the prosperity and cultural revival of the later Middle Ages, with its lively interest in making and wearing stylish jewelry.

# 4

# The Romanesque and Gothic Eras (A.D. 1000 to 1450)

The second half of the Middle Ages was a time of recovery and growth. Western Europe rested and rebuilt itself for a couple of centuries after the marauding barbarians settled down to become peaceful peasants and semi-peaceful knights and barons. Roman Catholicism asserted itself throughout western Europe, great monasteries were founded, and cathedrals and castles were built, around which towns began to grow. After that, Europe enjoyed a gradual revival of commerce and learning, and as wealth and cosmopolitanism increased, a new sort of jewelry appeared that was a pleasing union of the barbarian, Byzantine, and Greco-Roman traditions.

## The Age of Faith

The wimple and veil, a headdress that covered a woman's head (except for her face), throat, and breast, as well as the religious fervor of the times, made the interval between the years 1000 and 1250 a discouraging time both for those who made jewelry and for those who might have liked to wear it. This Romanesque era, so-called because the architecture of the period drew heavily on Roman and Byzantine conventions, saw enthusiastic crusading, the rise of great monastic orders, and the establishment of the Holy Roman Empire, but nothing that would inspire a lady to take off her muffle of veils and commission a pearl and sapphire necklace.

Feudalism, which focused on the production of food and other basic resources by peasants bound to and supervised by local nobles, became the dominant social and economic system. With life centering around small, agricultural fiefdoms and a barter economy that depended on payment in goods rather than coin, there was little money in circulation to spend on personal adornment, and men and women in any case had little incentive to dress extravagantly or wear fine jewels.

# Romanesque Jewelry Making

Very little jewelry from the Romanesque era has survived into modern times, mainly because very little was made or worn, as can be seen from paintings and sculpture of the period. Women's dress from A.D. 1000 to 1250 was extremely modest (it became the model for the traditional nun's habit) and not conducive to wearing necklaces, bracelets, or earrings. Because garments were sewn, even brooches became less essential to a woman's wardrobe, though she might use them singly to fasten the throat of her undertunic or in a pair, linked by a band of cloth, to fasten her cloak. These were usually ring brooches. Her belt, although otherwise unadorned, might include a chatelain—an assortment of implements in gold, silver, or bronze, linked together on a ring, for use in her housekeeping duties and personal grooming.

Most jewelry that was made failed to survive the centuries, mainly because, as Gregorietti writes, "Christian burial rites, by then in general use, put an end to the tradition of burying the dead with all their wealth and jewels."[27]

Jewelry generally had a function other than personal adornment; for example, men's seal rings, the equivalent of a legal signature in an age when most people could not read and write. Most jewelry consisted of royal and religious ornaments. "The most interesting pieces of goldware which have come down to us are almost exclusively important pieces which were preserved in cathedral, abbey, or royal treasuries."[28]

Crowns and other regalia were made, but goldsmiths were mainly kept busy with book covers, reliquaries, portable altars, and similar items for the Church. Gregorietti notes, "With rare exceptions the services of goldsmiths were completely monopolised by the Church and, therefore, hardly any jewelry was made for the laity."[29]

The influence on Romanesque jewelry is principally Byzantine, with barbaric and Greco-Roman elements added in, sometimes in rather surprising ways: "It is not uncommon to

## RELIGIOUS JEWELS

With Europe's conversion to Christianity came the passion for religious amulets and reliquaries. Those who could indulge in such things did so lavishly. Charlemagne, king of the Franks, owned a jeweled reliquary shaped like a pilgrim's flask, set with two enormous cabochon sapphires back to back. Between them was a piece of wood said to be from the cross on which Jesus Christ was crucified.

One type of religious jewelry, which might or might not contain a sacred relic, was the sort that opened, either to show internal leaves like a little book, delicately enameled, or the triptych pendant on which a pair of doors opened to reveal a scene inside, either enameled or, in particularly rich examples, carved on a cameo as in the lovely Nativity triptych.

An especially interesting example of the leaved type is the Holy Thorn Reliquary. It is a small, bean-shaped pendant that opens to show three panels (the two outer leaves and one side of the middle one) richly enameled with scenes from the life of Jesus Christ and a barefoot king kneeling in prayer. The fourth panel is covered with a parchment painting of the Nativity that lifts out to reveal a tiny compartment holding a thorn from Christ's crown of thorns.

find a bishop's ring set with a gem engraved with a pagan subject, in strong contrast to Catholic principles."[30] The example Gregorietti gives is set with a lovely intaglio of a nude goddess. The enamelwork, filigree, and massed pearls and polished but uncut colored stones popular in Byzantine times continued to be used, but the workmanship was often even cruder than during the Byzantine era, mainly because in the chaos of the early Middle Ages, many of the skills of classical Greek and Byzantine jewelers had been forgotten throughout much of western Europe, and goldsmiths learned however they could.

Fine jewelry did continue to be made in southern Italy and Sicily. One very lovely example of such work was the crown of Queen Constanza of Sicily.

# The Crown of Queen Constanza

In spite of invasions by Ostrogoths, Lombards, and Normans, Italy and Sicily maintained close ties with Byzantium and the eastern Mediterranean, and the jewels produced by Italian goldsmiths were of high quality. The royal palace workshops at Palermo, which provided regalia for the Norman rulers of the Kingdom of Sicily, attracted Greek and Middle Eastern craftsmen as well as Italians, and the pieces they turned out were masterful. Such is the crown found in the tomb of Constanza of Aragon, Spanish queen of Frederick II of Sicily, in the cathedral at Palermo.

Although the crown was buried with Constanza, who died in 1222, the style and workmanship suggest that it is a much earlier piece, dating from around 1130. Its influence is backward-looking, strongly Byzantine. In fact, it is patterned on the Byzantine imperial crown: a meshwork skullcap around which is fixed a band encircling the wearer's head and supporting two arching bands that cross over the top. These bands are decorated with four-lobed enameled plaques, each set with a large polished gemstone, alternating with large pearls. Bands, plaques, and pearls are outlined with a double row of seed pearls. Additional gemstones adorn the areas between the bands. The

stones are predominantly sapphires, and the overall effect is of glistening blue on a field of gold frosted with seed pearls.

One curious feature of the crown is the decoration on the border, which Gregorietti describes as "sixteen finely punched gold stylised lilies in the oriental manner, each with a little turquoise in the centre."[31] The lily "in the oriental manner," although Middle Eastern in origin, was at this point the badge of the Norman kings of Sicily. It appears later in the fleur-de-lis crest of the French royal dynasties, perhaps passed along through Norman connections.

It is unusual to find gold meshwork in a piece of jewelry from this period. Perhaps the technique was kept alive in the Muslim East and brought to Palermo by Muslim craftsmen.

# The Gothic Flowering

From about 1250 on, a combination of factors—a ferment of ideas brought back from the Middle East by returning crusaders and the reestablishment of trade throughout the Mediterranean—undermined the feudal system and fostered the rise of cities and universities. The result was a culture not only urban but urbane, with a thriving monetary economy. It rapidly turned into a goldsmith's dream.

# Jewelry Making in the Gothic Era

The Gothic era, which began around A.D. 1250, emerged out of the Romanesque like an enchanted tree. Its architecture soared upward with lacy fantasies and fantastic monsters, and in the relatively settled security of the times, its decorative arts turned once again toward the beauties of the natural world. As British art historian Joan Evans writes, "The early fourteenth century was a time of delicate lyricism in all the decorative arts. The love of romance that found expression in amatory inscriptions, the feeling for natural beauty that was expressed in every art from monumental sculpture to illumination and embroidery, the taste for a rather mannered elegance, were all reflected in the design of jewels."[32]

The rise of cities stimulated a thriving middle class; elegant, city-bred courtiers replaced country barons; and the wealth flowing in from the renewal of trade tempted goldsmiths back to a thriving trade in jewelry making. In the larger cities guilds were formed to train members of the craft and regulate the quality of the pieces made. For the first time a distinction was made between goldsmiths and "jewelers," craftsmen who specialized in cutting, shaping, and polishing gemstones. By the 1300s the wearing of jewelry by both men and women had become so popular that rulers started passing (and repealing) laws governing which social classes could wear what sorts of jewelry. It seems likely that these laws were not very rigorously enforced.

In the Gothic era jewelry, such as this ring brooch set with cabochon rubies and sapphires, became more ornamental than functional.

Gemstones were still cabochon, polished and to some degree shaped (ovals, rectangles, or lozenges) but without faceting, and the cutting and polishing usually followed the shape of the stone. Diamonds began to be used; they were not faceted, but simple point and table cuts using the natural shape of the diamond crystal appeared around 1400. Cameos and intaglios were prized, and medieval

craftsmen often reused Greco-Roman pieces, though cameo carving continued in Byzantium from Greco-Roman times onward, and fine ones, such as the Noah Cameo, were being made in Italy and Sicily as early as 1200.

Jewelry after 1250 became more ornamental than functional. Women as well as men began to wear rings set with pearls and precious gems in fanciful settings, and a nobleman's rings were not just his father's legal signature anymore, although seal rings with intaglio gems or engraved gold signets continued to be worn. Duke John the Fearless of Burgundy sported a ring with a tall, goblet-shaped bezel flanked on either side with a dragon's head rising from a collar of fleurs-de-lis; he also owned one with a portrait of himself in carved ivory, enamel, and precious stones set in gold. He may have worn them together; it became the fashion of those who could afford it to wear several rings on each hand and even more than one on a finger.

## Brooches, Brooches, Brooches

The functional ring brooch of Romanesque times continued to be worn, though by the 1300s it was considered somewhat out of fashion. Among the moneyed and fashion-conscious the ring brooch evolved into hexagonal and heart shapes, decorated with niello prayers and romantic sentiments or enamel and filigree flowers. Those that retained the original ring shape were enriched with praying hands, gems in tall cone-shaped settings called collets, or delicate reliefs in the form of leaves, flowers, and fruit.

Other types of circular brooch evolved from the ring brooch, with the sort of pin and catch used on brooches today. The wheel brooch consisted of one or more rings connected by "spokes," rings and spokes decorated with gems or gold work. The cluster brooch was a circular brooch with a single large jewel in the center, surrounded by pearls or other smaller gems. Brooches were made in other shapes as well; for example, the lozenge, like the Fleur-de-Lis Brooch, a diamond-shaped plaque with gold fleurs-de-lis on a blue enamel background, on which is set a single large fleur-de-lis set with precious stones.

Most elaborate of all are brooches that incorporate sculptural elements cast using the lost wax method and usually richly enameled. The Founder's Jewel, bequeathed to New College, Oxford, by its founder William of Wykeham in 1404, is a monogram letter M in which the two spaces formed by the arches of the letter are transformed into two Gothic niches in which stand beautifully modeled and enameled figures of the Angel of the Annunciation and the Madonna. Between them, the central stroke of the letter supports a vase carved from a ruby, from which spring three enameled lilies. The rest of the letter is richly encrusted with gems and pearls. An equally striking example is the Lovers Brooch from around 1450, depicting a pair of lovers in a garden. The boy and girl are cast, and decorated with blue and white enamel; the boy's hair is done in coiling gold wire. They stand in a garden of enameled green leaves and tiny pearl flowers in high relief, surrounded by a paling fence that forms the outer rim of the brooch, which is also decorated with a triangular diamond, a ruby, and several large pearls.

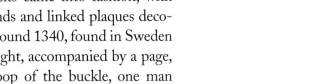

The heart-shaped brooch was fashionable in the Gothic era.

## Belts and Necklaces

Around 1340, elaborate jeweled belts came into fashion, with beautifully cast buckles and strap ends and linked plaques decorated with enamel. A buckle from around 1340, found in Sweden but probably German, depicts a knight, accompanied by a page, riding to meet his lady. On the loop of the buckle, one man kneels to another in a bower of grapevines. Men and women wore both waist and hip belts, and also wide, baldric-style belts that went over one shoulder and under the opposite arm.

Among noble ladies, hair and headdresses went up and necklines came down, exposing throats and bosoms to be adorned with fine necklaces. (Earrings, however, did not catch on because the headdresses and hairstyles of the late Middle

# THE GOLDSMITH

**D**uring the Gothic era most goldsmiths worked in cities and had their shops in one central location, often on bridges like the Ponte Vecchio in Florence, where there was a regular flow of traffic. They belonged to guilds, which were something between a labor union and a professional association; the guild fixed prices, set quality standards, and oversaw the training of apprentices.

A boy training to become a goldsmith served an apprenticeship with a master goldsmith. Although his father was often a goldsmith, the boy was usually apprenticed to another goldsmith in the same guild. The boy's father or sponsor had to put up a bond so that the master would be reimbursed if the apprentice proved unsatisfactory. The apprentice lived with the master and his family and trained in the master's shop. Once the master was satisfied with his progress, he was promoted to journeyman. (The term "journeyman" comes from the French word *jour*, meaning "day," because the journeyman was paid by the day.) Though free to seek employment elsewhere many journeymen remained with their master and even married into his family. When he was judged advanced enough the journeyman made his "master piece"; if the guild passed on it he became a master goldsmith in his own right.

Ages usually covered the ears.) Both sexes wore "collars," which might be anything from the choker sort of necklaces seen on ladies in the Duke de Berry's books of hours (a type of personal prayer book) to the massive, shoulder-width chains, often with a pendant, worn by noblemen over their outer robes. When the French princess Isabelle de Valois came to England in 1396 to marry Richard II, her enchanted husband-to-be presented her with, among other rich gifts, "a collar of diamonds, rubies and large pearls."[33] Necklaces, too, remained in fashion.

Above all, jewelry of the Gothic era was characterized by a kind of fanciful delicacy. No piece of Gothic jewelry is more typical of the airy grace of the period than the Crown of Princess Blanche.

# A Princess's Wedding Crown

This fairy-tale crown is called the Crown of Princess Blanche because it was sent with Blanche of Lancaster, daughter of Henry IV of England, to be worn at her wedding in 1404. But in fact it was rifled from the treasury of Richard II when Henry IV usurped his throne in 1399 and sent him off to imprisonment and murder. It was originally part of the trousseau of little Princess Isabelle de Valois whom Richard married in 1396.

It is the perfect crown for a little bride who is also a princess, as different as can be from the squat Byzantine diadems of the Romanesque era such as the crown of Queen Constanza. From a garland of rubies, sapphires, and pearl-and-emerald blossoms, twelve slender spires rise up like the columns of a Gothic cathedral, ending in Gothic ivy leaves, each centered with a sapphire and tipped with a pearl ornament. From the sides of the spires, smaller leaves branch out, framing sapphires and pearl flowers. It is so delicate it looks almost weightless, as if it would float above the little princess's head whenever she wore it.

Between 1450 and 1500, the dreamlike elegance of the Gothic era surged into the very wide-awake vigor of the Renaissance, which was both a journey back to Greek and Roman learning and artistic values and a journey forward to the riches and adventure of a new world. All this energy had a great impact on the style of Renaissance jewelry.

# 5

# The Renaissance
# (A.D. 1450 to 1600)

The Renaissance, which means "rebirth," began in Italy and spread across Europe to the north and west. It grew naturally out of the revival of learning during the late Middle Ages, as the works of Greek and Roman authors made their way into the hands of secular scholars by way of the great universities at Solerno and Bologna, Paris, Heidelberg, and Oxford. Shortly after 1450, printed books appeared, which made the written word available to anyone who could read and greatly advanced the spread of knowledge across Europe. With the growing enthusiasm for classical (Greek and Roman) learning came a return to classical humanism—the recognition of the human mind and body as beautiful and admirable. This way of thinking had an effect on jewelry, which came to be viewed as a means of enhancing and celebrating the human body. Writes art historian Daniela Mascetti,

> The transition from Gothic styles to those of the Renaissance was largely prompted by a renewed interest in the culture and arts of Ancient Greece and Rome. . . . It was . . . the rediscovery of human beauty in the nude, and the recognition of man as an individ-

ual whose natural dignity springs from his qualities and merits, which were the most immediate influences on fashion and jewelry. Clothes and jewels became a means of enhancing natural human beauty, rather than overshadowing it with artificiality, thus establishing a new harmony between body, dress and ornament.[34]

But the great discoveries of the Renaissance focused on the future as well as the past. In 1492 a Genoese sea captain named Christopher Columbus stepped ashore on the island of San Salvador in the Bahamas and opened up a whole new world to Europeans. With the discovery of the Americas vast wealth poured into Europe, plundered from the native peoples: gold and silver from priceless Aztec and Inca works of art melted down into bars, precious stones from Mexico and the Andes. With these riches came a spirit of adventure, exploration, and conquest that also influenced Renaissance jewelry, in the self-confident naturalism and exuberant imagination it expressed.

Renaissance jewelry drew on classical sculpture and the general humanistic and expansive spirit of the age rather than on Greek and Roman jewelry itself. Except for surviving cameos and intaglios, Greco-Roman jewelry was virtually unknown and never copied. As Evans writes, "Apart from the imitation of antique cameos, there seems to have been little direct classical influence: neither the technique of filigree nor the style of jewels all of delicate gold were revived."[35]

This portrait of Simonetta Vespucci captures how women wore their hair in fantastic braids and knots interwoven with jewels.

# The Renaissance Jeweler's Art

With the celebration of the human body came an enthusiasm for adorning it. Jewelry in all forms, with beautiful and elaborate designs, became popular. From the Italian painter Botticelli's goddesses to state portraits of Queen Elizabeth I, Renaissance ladies were festooned with gold chains, ropes of pearls, and strands of precious stones. In Italy hair once again became a woman's crowning glory, and it was worn in soft waves and fantastic braids and knots interwoven with jewels. Simonetta Vespucci, a reigning Florentine beauty, was painted by both Botticelli and Piero di Cosimo with her flowing blond hair worn in this fashion. A portrait of apple-cheeked little Barbara Pallavicino shows her wearing a Juliet hairnet, a jeweled circlet, and a large emerald and pearl hair ornament.

In the north of Europe, the parure, a lavish set of matching jewels, came into fashion. It might include one or more necklaces, pendants, and brooches as well as jeweled bands to decorate the low, square neckline and the headdress. Ladies commonly wore two necklaces, a short collar, or carcanet, and a longer plain or jeweled chain or rope of pearls draped over the shoulders, either or both of which might support a pendant. They might also wear a brooch in the center of the bodice, as seen in Hans Holbein's portrait of Jane Seymour. Queen Elizabeth I in the Ditchley portrait wears, in addition to a three-strand, long necklace of pearls and a knotted rope of pearls, a carcanet of alternating ruby and emerald settings separated by florettes of pearls; a matching bodice ornament; large pearls and plaques sewn all over her gown, complementing her carcanet; pearl, ruby, and emerald hair ornaments; and a coronet tipped with an emerald and an enormous ruby that resemble an olive and a cherry tomato on a toothpick.

Men as well as women sported parures of gems designed to complement their rich clothing. As Gregorietti says, "Forms and colours had to be in harmonious accord or contrast with the colours of the fabrics."[36] In Holbein's portrait of Henry VIII, from whom Elizabeth I, his daughter, inherited her taste for extravagant jewels, the king wears an elaborate wide chain draped over his shoulders. "The chain is the same as the one designed by Holbein now in the British museum, London; it consists of knotted elements finely modelled with buds, leaves, and scrolls set with large, table-cut rubies in embellished mounts. Between each gem are set two pearls."[37] The king's finger rings, as well as his jeweled buttons, hat ornaments, and the clasps that fasten the slashings on his sleeves are designed to match the ensemble.

This portrait of Queen Elizabeth I exemplifies the parure, or set of matching jewels. All of the jewelry on her body, on her dress, and in her hair matches or is complementary.

Both men and women wore rings, often more than one on a hand. These were delicately adorned with niello or enameled, often on the inside as well as the outside, and set with gems or pearls. Signet rings remained popular, with either engraved gems or gold bezels carved with coats of arms or classical subjects. An interesting Renaissance fashion was the ring with a hinged lid that opened to reveal a small compartment; though these are popularly referred to today as "poison rings," they were most likely containers for religious relics and other religious objects.

Earrings made a tentative comeback in the Renaissance. They were more popular with men than with women, because women's hairstyles and headdresses still tended to cover the ears. They did not really become popular with women until the 1600s.

It was no accident that all these fashions in jewels were so elegant. Famous artists were in demand as designers of jewelry. Holbein, best known for his portraits of King Henry VIII and his queens, also turned his hand to sketching patterns for their

# THE SWASHBUCKLER: BENVENUTO CELLINI

Most of what we know about Benvenuto Cellini (1500–1571), goldsmith, musician, soldier, and rascal, he tells us himself in his autobiography. And what an autobiography it is. The Web site Answers.com reports that "Cellini tells of his escapades with the frankness and consummate egoism characteristic of the Renaissance man."[1] Between his battles, rivalries, amorous interludes, and occasional murders, it is amazing that the man had time to get any work done at all. But he did. Expert Joan Evans in *A History of Jewelry, 1100–1870* calls him "the type of the Renaissance jewellers who by sheer virtuosity attained the rank of artist."[2]

No jewels survive today that are known to be his work, although a lovely medallion of Leda and the Swan is attributed to him. Among his known surviving works is a famous salt cellar depicting the gods of earth and sea that he made for the king of France.

Today a portrait bust of Cellini is enshrined on the Ponte Vecchio, still the Florentine jewelers' quarter, in tribute to Florence's most notorious master goldsmith.

1. Answers.com, "Benvenuto Cellini." www.answers.com.
2. Joan Evans, *A History of Jewelry, 1100–1870*. Boston: Boston Book and Art, 1970, p. 83.

collars and brooches and pendants. The studies that have survived are themselves small works of art. To all these lavish styles of jewelry making, Renaissance jewelers applied new techniques even as they refined old ones.

# Renaissance Jewelers' Techniques

New techniques in enameling that had begun in the late Middle Ages were continued and further developed in the Renaissance.

In the case of a very frequently used technique, enamel *champlevé*, the enamel is contained in beds gouged into the metal. *Basse-taille* enamel was translucent, added over a design engraved into the groundplate. A special technique used from the fourteenth century was called *ronde bosse* or painted enamel. The enamel was applied to previously roughened surfaces in high relief or even completely in the round. The so-called Dunstable Swan Jewel . . . is among the most famous examples of the use of *ronde bosse* enamelling.[38]

Renaissance gem cutters also expanded their craft. Europe had a ready supply of precious stones: raw turquoise and emeralds from the New World and diamonds, rubies, sapphires, and pearls that Portuguese merchants were bringing back from India and Ceylon. These provided craftsmen with a rich supply of gems with which to work.

During the Renaissance, gem shaping progressed to the point of producing gems of uniform shapes and sizes. Gem cutting, however, still followed the simple cabochon point and table cuts of the late Middle Ages, although diamond polishing improved greatly, and the point and table cuts began to be applied to colored stones as well as to diamonds. Still, applied to diamonds, the point and table cuts did not display the strong dispersion of light, or "fire," of a modern diamond. In the Renaissance, diamonds were valued for their lustrous surface rather than their inner sparkle; table-cut diamonds appear black to the eye, as they do in paintings and photographs.

Northern Italy, primarily Florence and later Rome and Venice, became the new center for the art of carving cameos and intaglios. Italian gem carvers were renowned for their skill, and they were hired away to courts all over Europe. Popes and noblemen collected their masterpieces. Some of the most fantastic examples of rich enamel work and the fanciful use of gems are the pendants and brooches made for wealthy Renaissance patrons.

# Make Me One with Everything: Renaissance Pendants and Brooches

Jeweled and enameled ships in full sail navigate across ladies' bosoms or hung from noblemen's gold collars. Mermaids and mermen cavort through the waves. A black-enameled African trudges across a landscape encrusted with rubies and emeralds, carrying a large basket of gems. A blue-enameled and baroque pearl salamander with an emerald pendant in his mouth writhes on intricate chains beneath a pearl pendant. In the making of pendants and brooches, the Renaissance goldsmith let his imagination run riot. And his patrons loved it.

Jewels with cast sculptural elements were very popular, as they were in the late Middle Ages, but the technique improved astronomically. As Evans writes, "Certain Renaissance jewels are such *tours de force* of minute sculpture that they have passed the line that divides art from virtuosity. Such reliefs . . . demand judgment as pure sculpture."[39]

Goldsmiths seemed challenged to see how many kinds of decoration they could fit onto a brooch or pendant. Enameled gold bases are encrusted with cut and cabochon and carved jewels, hung with jeweled and pearl pendants, fitted around monstrous baroque pearls.

Both goldsmiths and patrons especially loved the so-called baroque pearls (the name comes from Italian *barocco*, "imperfect pearl"), great misshapen nodules of mother-of-pearl that defied the imagination to see what could be made of them. They form the bodies of gods and mercreatures, dragons and monsters, and fabulous birds and beasts. One particular-

A Renaissance-era enameled gold pendant.

# THE RENAISSANCE CAMEO

Northern Italy was acknowledged by all of Europe to produce the greatest carvers of cameos and intaglios of the Renaissance. Their craft probably came from southern Italy, where it had flourished during the Middle Ages, but they brought to it the full zest of Renaissance humanism and a return to classical subjects: gods and goddesses, bacchanalian revels, shepherdesses and fauns. They also carved portraits of their patrons, some of whom made collections of their works.

Cameos in this time were hard stone carvings. Some were done in stones such as carnelian and jasper, but the preferred stone was a banded onyx or agate, in which the figures could be carved in relief against a contrasting background. Usually the figures were light on dark, but as the Age of Exploration excited a taste for the exotic, black figures were carved against a light background, as in a striking African Diana.

The Renaissance enthusiasm for variety influenced cameo carving and inspired craftsmen to add embellishments such as the Black Diana's gold-and-pearl earring. Sometimes the cameo carving was set against a background of gold or enamel instead of the matrix of its native stone, as in the lovely composite cameos by Ottavio Miseroni or Cellini's Leda.

ly knobbly specimen hangs as a bunch of grapes from a jeweled and enameled mounting.

The results are jewels of exuberant fantasy. Two pieces, one a pendant and one a brooch, particularly capture the modern imagination. One is the pendant known as the Canning Jewel, which features a belligerent merman armed with sword and shield. The Canning merman's torso is formed from a monstrous baroque pearl. His head, arm, tail, and shield are of gold, enameled opaque white and blue and a translucent green that shows scales incised into the underlying groundwork. His tail, belt, sword, and shield are set with table-cut diamonds and cabochon rubies; the large carved ruby in the middle of his body may be a later addition. Three large baroque pearl pendants hang from the merman's body and shield to give the piece balance. The overall effect expresses perfectly the merman's princely courage and bravado.

The other, a brooch that once belonged to the Grand Duke of Tuscany, features a rooster. One theme of Renaissance pendants and brooches was birds. Normally, these were birds with either noble or exotic associations, such as swans, eagles, pelicans, or parrots. This particular cockerel, known affectionately as the "Florentine Rooster,"[40] may be one of the many cases of a Florentine artist celebrating the feisty underdog that symbolized the city of Florence. He is a remarkably handsome little fellow. His body is of gold, built around a large baroque pearl that forms his throat and hackle. His head, wings, and lower body are richly enameled in iridescent green and blue and opaque white. He has a cabochon ruby eye; he wears a point-cut ruby on his breast and another large ruby set into his wing, and his red, green, and blue tail feathers are studded with table-cut diamonds. His green-enameled feet tread an enameled scepter underfoot.

These jewels express the spirit of the Renaissance, which mingled the art and the humanism of Greece and Rome with its own exuberance. The period that followed was a curious echo of Byzantium: stately, pompous, unimaginative, and very concerned with maintaining the status quo, all of which had a quelling effect on the jewels that people wore.

# 6

# Baroque and Rococo (A.D. 1600 to 1815)

By around 1600 the bold self-confidence of the Renaissance seemed to settle into a period of stifling self-importance. This baroque era was an age of the divine right of kings. Kings and nobles enjoyed absolute power over the people; Louis XIV informed the French parliament, "L'état, c'est moi!" ("I am the State!") This absolutism was most extreme in France, although the rest of Europe followed its example.

Around 1700 France dissolved into the giddy gaiety of the rococo era. French queen Marie Antoinette went to balls in diamond-studded slippers, while the common people suffered famine and groaned under the authority of the nobles. If the harvest was bad, as it often was in these years of exhausted soil and exhausted peasantry, the king and nobles took their share regardless. Shortages drove up the price of grain, and both peasants and urban poor went hungry. Marie Antoinette probably never said "Let them eat cake" when she was told that the people of Paris were angry because they had no bread. There is no question, however, that the poor women of Paris marched on the royal palace at Versailles to protest their own suffering and the greed and indifference of the noble class.

As it followed the French example in government, the rest of Europe also followed the French example in fashion, and particularly in the fashions of jewelry. The jewelry of these times ranged from the icy formality of the baroque to the glittering excesses of rococo. Inspired by the early regime of Napoléon, it ended in a stern neoclassicism that copied the styles of ancient classical jewelry.

## Pomp and Pompousness

Kings and nobles, who wore the jewelry in the baroque era, were full of pompous self-regard. In fact they swelled with it as their clothing and hats and wigs billowed to the point that their jewelry was quite dwarfed and overshadowed. The jewelry itself was curiously static compared to the explosive imagination of the Renaissance. Its principal inspirations seem to have been the formal gardens and monumental architecture that symbolized the majesty of the king and nobility.

## Baroque Jewelry Making

Baroque jewelry emphasized faceted gems, particularly diamonds, instead of the brilliant gold work and enameling of the Renaissance. The stones were arranged in linear rows and rigid geometric clusters. Motifs were few and unimaginative: scrolls, feathers, formalized leaves and flowers, ribbon bows. Gold work and enameling became little more than a background on which to display the gems.

One reason for this dramatic change in style was the rapid development in cutting and faceting diamonds. In the late Renaissance, diamond cutters in Antwerp invented the rose cut, a flat-bottomed crown with perfectly symmetrical triangular facets. Around 1650 the first brilliant diamond cut was introduced, which displayed the diamond's fire as well as its luster. Known as the Mazarin, it had a table and sixteen facets on the crown (upper part) of the stone. A Venetian polisher named Peruzzi increased the number of facets on the crown to thirty-two, in what is known as the Peruzzi cut. These diamonds showed infinitely more fire than the old point and table cuts, but

the Mazarin and Peruzzi cuts, because of their rectangular shape, were rather dull compared to modern round-cut diamonds.

Other precious stones also began to be faceted to match the diamond, and, says Gregorietti, "From the second half of the century onwards, precious personal ornaments were dominated by faceted gems, and it became inconceivable to mount cabochon stones. . . . The principal place in the design was given to precious stones cut in various shapes and sizes."[41]

The other reason for the preference for stones over gold work was a steady supply of diamonds and other precious stones imported from India. Although the Portuguese had dominated the trade in oriental gems during the Renaissance, by the 1600s the British, Dutch, and French East India Companies were edging them out, and adventurers like Jean-Baptiste de Tavernier made a career out of the diamond trade.

The result was a steadily increasing flow of not only diamonds but also rubies, sapphires, and pearls from the East.

Pearls were the most popular gem after the diamond. They were set with diamonds and used almost offhandedly as decorations on jewels featuring other gems. Strands of pearls were also popular at the time. Says Mascetti, "Undoubtedly, . . . the most fashionable form of neck ornament throughout the century was the pearl necklace."[42] The pearl necklace was a constant with both noble ladies and the wealthy middle class, and the drop-shaped pearl, either by itself or with other gems as embellishments, was worn in earrings, as in Dutch painter Jan Vermeer's immortal *Girl with a Pearl Earring*.

The drop-shaped pearl earring is showcased in Jan Vermeer's famous work *Girl with a Pearl Earring*.

## Ribbons and Bows

The one really distinctive jewelry motif of the 1600s was the ribbon bow. Necklaces were fastened with ribbon ties fed through loops on the ends and tied in a bow, as in Vermeer's famous painting of the lady tying on her pearl necklace. This sort of fastening allowed the wearer to adjust the tightness of the necklace to ride fashionably high on the throat. Bows were also used to attach pendants to earrings and generally to fasten clothing. Gradually these ribbon-bow elements were themselves translated into fashion accessories rather than functional fastenings, and ultimately into jewelry in the shape of ribbon bows.

Ribbon bows went from functional fastenings to fashion accessories.

One enterprising enameler capitalized on the trend of making necklaces of linked gold or silver bows: "Necklaces of this type frequently featured polychrome painted enamel decoration, a technique developed in the early decades of the century by the French jeweler, Jean Toutin (1578–1640), to produce opaque white or pale blue backgrounds with black decoration or vice versa."[43] Judging from surviving examples, the effect was lacy and quite elegant. Toutin also extended his enamel-painting technique to making portrait miniatures.

## Glitter and Greed

If baroque jewels shimmered and glowed, rococo jewels flashed and glittered and sparkled. This was the era in which the diamond came into its own. Necklaces and brooches and bracelets and rings were designed almost entirely to show off the fire of diamonds.

# THE CURSE OF THE HOPE DIAMOND

It is unlikely that Jean-Baptiste de Tavernier stole the great blue diamond from the forehead of an Indian idol and so brought a curse to anyone who owned it. It is true that Tavernier brought the stone back from India and sold it to King Louis XIV. Louis XIV did not suffer any ill effects from owning the diamond, but his descendants died in tragically large numbers at tragically early ages. Louis XVI, who inherited the stone, had his life cut short by the guillotine during the French Revolution. The diamond, known as the French Blue, was stolen in 1791 and disappeared.

In 1823 a large blue diamond thought to be a recut of the French Blue turned up in London. Eventually it came into the possession of Henry Philip Hope, a wealthy collector who gave the diamond its present name. After his death the diamond was sold to a succession of buyers who suffered various misfortunes. Finally, it was bought by New York diamond merchant Harry Winston, who donated it to the Smithsonian Institution in 1958. Winston, who died of natural causes at the age of eighty-two, did not believe in the curse of the Hope Diamond.

The Hope Diamond pendant.

# Rococo Jewelry Making

The rococo era, which extended from around 1700 to the collapse of the French monarchy with the French Revolution in 1789, was a time of eccentric frivolity and the absolute rule of French fashion throughout Europe; and French fashion decreed diamonds, diamonds, and more diamonds. While hairdos rose to ridiculous heights and skirts spread out until two ladies could not pass through a door together, the plunging neckline and the diamonds that set it off remained a fashionable constant.

Very few actual examples of rococo diamond jewelry have survived intact, because diamonds, as valuable as they are, are recut and reset to accommodate the fashions of later times. Fortunately, enough noble ladies of the 1700s sat for their portraits in their diamond parures that it is possible to see how rococo diamond jewelry looked.

By the 1700s metal settings had become virtually invisible and served almost entirely as a support for diamonds and other gems. Diamonds were set in silver so that the setting would not contrast with the color of the stones, and the silver itself was backed with gold plating or fabric so that it would not discolor the wearer's skin and clothing with black tarnish.

Two factors accounted for the diamond's enormous popularity. First, by the early 1700s diamond cutters began to develop the modern round brilliant cut. The early form of this cut, which remained in use throughout the 1800s and was known as the old European, had a more rounded shape than the earlier Mazarin and Peruzzi cuts and was also "a cut that enhanced the optical properties of diamonds and enabled the stone to reflect light and sparkle."[44]

Second, the popularity of the diamond was enhanced by the discovery of large deposits in Brazil just as the diamond fields in India were running out; diamonds were in good supply, readily available to those who could afford them.

# Rococo Fashions in Jewelry

For the most part the motifs used in rococo jewelry were those of the previous century: geometric forms, feathers, stylized

leaves and flowers, the ribbon bow. Although colored stones came back into vogue around 1760, color schemes were flat—generally diamonds with at most one or two additional colors. The color scheme was usually carried throughout a lady's parure of matching pieces.

The focal piece of a lady's parure was the necklace, which was worn high about the throat to emphasize the slenderness and elegance of the wearer's neck. Two styles were particularly popular: the band necklace and the rivière. The former consisted of

an articulated open-work band of varying width set with a variety of gemstones. This basic form could be enriched by the addition of a central pendant either in the shape of a ribbon bow or a cross. Alternatively, it could support a pendant designed as a pear-shaped drop or an elaborate combination of ribbon bow and drops. . . . The most elaborate version of this type of necklace was known as the *esclavage*, which consisted of the basic open-work band embellished with single or multiple central festoons [looped swags], often enriched with pendants. All these additional elements could be detached from the basic band by means of a hook-and-eye device, making this type of neck ornament particularly versatile.[45]

The rivière (a "river" of gems) was a single line of large gemstones, often graduated in size from the middle, usually supporting a large diamond drop. The gemstones might be diamonds or colored gems, often surrounded with smaller diamonds. With

The aigrette, shown here as a brooch, was an ornament in the shape of a spray of egret feathers, used to adorn a lady's hair or clothing.

the necklace went matching earrings with faceted drops or a girandole design, which had three pendants attached to a single large diamond or an ornate base. If the lady desired and could afford it, she also wore matching bracelets, rings, brooches, and jeweled hair ornaments. Gregorietti describes a portrait of an Italian noblewoman of the period:

> She wears a rich *parure* of diamonds consisting of an *aigrette* [an ornament in the shape of a spray of egret feathers], together with at least seven other jewels scattered in her hair, as well as earrings made of three round gems set in a triangular shape with briolette pendants, and a diamond collar necklace made of curved elements matching those of the bracelet. In addition to rings, she has a long pearl necklace pinned to the left side of her décolleté by an *aigrette* brooch.[46]

Naturally all these diamond adornments were very costly. Noble ladies lavished a great deal of money on them, whether they could afford to or not. Such frivolous and extravagant displays did not sit well with the common people, who watched their children go hungry while aristocrats went to balls glittering and sparkling with jewels. When the queen of France herself created a scandal trying to acquire an elaborate diamond necklace (or so the rumor went), the results had long-reaching consequences for the royalty and aristocracy, as well as for France itself.

# The Queen's Necklace

French queen Marie Antoinette's passion for diamonds sparked a scandal in 1785 that shook the French monarchy to its foundations and paved the way for the Revolution that would overthrow it. The cause of all the trouble was a necklace of the more extreme *esclavage* ("slave") type that King Louis XV, grandfather-in-law of Marie Antoinette, commissioned for his mistress, Madame du Barry. The necklace, says Gregorietti, "consisted of a collar of seventeen huge diamonds from which were suspended three festoons

and four pendants entirely of diamonds; it was completed with another double rivière with four tassels also in diamonds."[47]

Louis XV died before the necklace was finished and paid for, and the designers, not wanting to find themselves out of pocket, offered it to King Louis XVI, Marie Antoinette's husband, who said he could not afford it. Some time later a shady character who called herself the Comtesse de la Motte persuaded the Cardinal de Rohan, who badly wanted to gain the queen's good graces, to buy the necklace for Marie Antoinette without Louis' knowledge. The cardinal was told the queen would pay him for

# THE TRAVELER: JEAN-BAPTISTE DE TAVERNIER

From an early age, Jean-Baptiste de Tavernier (1605–1689) wanted to travel. Perhaps the fact that his father and uncle were geographers had something to do with it. In 1630, having journeyed to Italy, Switzerland, Germany, Poland, and Hungary, he set out for the East with two French priests and reached Persia by way of Constantinople.

In 1638 he journeyed to India and visited the court of the Great Mogul. Impressed by the diamond mines at Golconda, he set himself up as a gentleman merchant dealing in precious gems. In all, he made five expeditions to the East, on one of them going as far as Java. He established profitable trade relations with the great potentates of India and acquired great wealth and a great reputation back in France. He sold the large blue diamond that became the Hope Diamond to Louis XIV, who made him a nobleman. In his late fifties he decided to marry, settle down, and spend his remaining years writing an account of his travels.

Perhaps the settled life did not agree with him. In 1687 he set off again, traveling to Moscow by way of Copenhagen. He died as he had lived most of his life, on the road.

the necklace. The trusting cardinal acquired the necklace and handed it over to the comtesse, who dispatched it to England to be broken up and sold. The ensuing scandal caused the cardinal to be exiled to his abbey, all thoughts of royal favor despaired of; the comtesse, after a brief imprisonment, moved on to more devious adventures.

Most historians agree that Marie Antoinette was not involved in the transaction. At the time, however, because of the queen's notorious extravagance, the people believed that she selfishly tried to acquire the necklace despite the fact that France could not afford it. The scandal fed revolutionary grumblings to overthrow a monarchy so insensitive to the needs of the people. The rococo era came to a bloody end in 1789 with the French Revolution, which overthrew the French monarchy and aristocracy and sent them to the guillotine.

# The Empire

With the French Revolution and the downfall of the French monarchy came the rejection of everything that had stood for rococo French fashion in the court of Louis XVI and Marie Antoinette. Taking advantage of the chaos that followed the Revolution, Napoléon Bonaparte siezed power in 1799. His regime began as a return to the democratic ideals of Greece and Rome.

Fashion followed society's return to classical ideals. Women turned to wearing what they imagined Greek clothing must have looked like: very simple, clinging, high-wasted gowns with low necklines. Jewelry too returned to a style called "neoclassical," inspired by classical Greece, with a renewed emphasis on gold work, simple lines, and a great interest in cameos, cabochon gems, and opaque colored stones that carried over into the next century.

Napoléon's regime ended with his downfall in 1815 after fifteen years of tyranny and imperial conquest throughout Europe. The world following the French Revolution and the final defeat of Napoléon's plans for empire was a world very different from the one of the 1600s and 1700s. It saw the Industrial Revolution, the rise of a solid middle class in both Europe and America, and a British queen who embodied the staunchest of middle-class values.

# 7

# The Victorians and Edwardians
# (A.D. 1815 to 1915)

Europe emerged from the horrors of the French Revolution and the Napoleonic Wars with a strong desire to settle down. This trend was accelerated by the Industrial Revolution, which gave rise to a thriving middle class that encouraged most European states to experiment with democracy or constitutional monarchy. England and the United States set the example. In the United States the Civil War (1861–1865) put an end to the country's last vestige of aristocratic society and the institution of black slavery that made it possible. In 1840 the young English queen Victoria married a proper German prince and dedicated herself to a life of respectability and good behavior that was to make her name a byword for middle-class virtue. Jewelry, while still lavish for formal and state occasions, was generally subdued and made of such materials and in such a way that most middle-class families could afford a bit of it.

Queen Victoria, who began her reign in 1837, was no frivolous and extravagant Marie Antoinette. Victoria's relentlessly middle-class virtues and domesticity had a great influence on fashions in general and jewelry in particular. Suddenly it was fashionable for even highly born ladies and gentlemen to dress modestly and wear modest and affordable jewelry.

# Queen Victoria's Influence on Style

Queen Victoria's personal tastes greatly influenced fashions in jewelry. The queen had a great admiration for things Scottish and started a vogue in Scottish jewelry—silver pieces in the form of antique Highland shoulder brooches, knots, buckles, crests, and swords, set with yellow or golden Cairngorm quartz gemstones and vividly colored, contrasting agates, often inlaid in intricate, very lovely quasi-plaid patterns that incorporated the natural banding of the stones. *Englishwoman's Domestic Magazine* in 1867 had this to say: "Scotch jewelry, as well as Scotch costume, is *de rigueur* and the badges of the different clans are worn as brooches, earrings, buckles and shoe rosettes."[48]

Victoria's marriage for love to her handsome cousin Prince Albert of Saxe-Coburg-Gotha made sentimentality and

During the Victorian era, jewelry pieces featuring flowers or a romantic love theme were in fashion.

romance fashionable, and with it a wide variety of sentimental jewelry. Parures in the style of "the fruiting vine"—emblem of married love and childbearing—and other symbolic plant and flower motifs were very popular: "Such necklaces . . . were largely indebted to the naturalistic motifs in favour at the time: clusters of fruit and berries alternating with leaves. Among the most common were those designed as fruiting vines. Entwined sprays of leaves and flowers such as ivy, orange blossoms, roses and forget-me-nots were also in vogue and were often used to symbolize love and affection."[49]

These motifs often played on the Language of Flowers. In an era when overt expressions of love were considered improper, lovers exchanged messages with one another by means of flowers, or jewelry in the shape of flowers, to each of which a special meaning was attached. This form of communication became known as the Language of Flowers.

In keeping with the reverence for married love, ladies wore simple gold or silver rings engraved or embossed with the word "Mizpah" as keeper rings for their wedding bands, symbolizing the biblical quotation, "The Lord watch between me and thee, when we are absent one from another" (Gen. 31:49). They were quite innocent of the real implications of the word in the original Bible passage: "For the narrative depicts Jacob and Laban, long suspicious of each other and here finding a special cause for mistrust, invoking God as a protection against the possible cupidity of the other. Further bearing out this meaning of the passage, the Hebrew word 'mizpah' means 'watch tower' and refers to a boundary marker to keep the two apart."[50]

When Albert gave his wife a necklace in the form of a serpent—symbol of wisdom, life, and eternity—with a heart-shaped pendant dangling from its jaws, snake jewelry, some of it modeled on Greek and Roman archaeological finds, became a fashionable necessity.

# Mourning Jewelry

After Albert's tragic death at the age of forty-one, Victoria went into deep mourning for him that continued for the rest of her

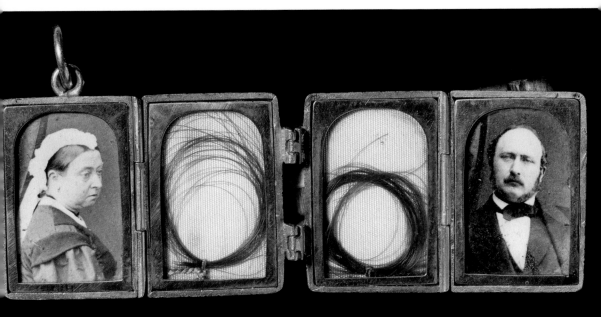

life, and mourning jewelry became a more or less enforced vogue. Ladies wore complete parures of glittering, faceted jet: "Materials such as jet were originally intended for mourning, but noteworthy people, such as Victorian opera singer Adelina Patti, made jet a desirable fashion accessory whether one was in mourning or not."[51]

A gold locket with portraits of Queen Victoria and Prince Albert, along with two locks of hair.

Portrait lockets, which had been in vogue for centuries, acquired a new popularity during Victorian times, especially after the advent of photography made it possible to enshrine a daguerreotype portrait of the beloved instead of the more costly painted miniature. These lockets, worn as pendants or brooches, became especially popular after the American Civil War, when many brothers, husbands, and fiancés met a premature death.

One peculiar manifestation of this preoccupation with death and mourning was jewelry made from hair of loved ones, living or deceased. Hair was most often woven into designs that were set in brooches and rings, but it was also sometimes used to make bracelets and necklaces.

# Jewelry Making for the Middle Class

During the Victorian era jewelry making for the middle class came into vogue. Industrial advances, such as steam-powered machines for stamping out gold and silver repoussé work, made jewelry less expensive. So did trends toward thinner, lighter settings that required less metal, and toward using cheaper materials such as semiprecious stones, glass, and even synthetic materials like gutta-percha, a hard rubber from which inexpensive cameolike settings were stamped. Lapis lazuli once again became popular, as did carnelian, malachite, and various sorts of agates.

Parures continued to be fashionable, and a distinction came to be made between the full parure, which consisted of matching necklace, earrings, bracelets, one or more brooches, and perhaps rings and buckles for belt and shoes, and the demi-parure, which consisted of two or three matching pieces.

# The Grand Tour

During the 1800s most well-off middle-class families could afford to vacation abroad, and railroads and steamships made traveling practical and pleasant. This middle-class migration coincided with the remarkable archaeological discoveries being made in Italy, where Pompeii and Herculaneum were beginning to be systematically excavated, as were Etruscan tombs. The result was that "Italy was the most popular destination for tourists, and . . . they . . . brought back substantial quantities of jewelry."[52]

Italian history, Italian archaeology, Italian art, Italian materials and artisans, and the wealth of the newly mobile middle class of America, Britain, and northern Europe combined to inspire some remarkable jewelry incorporating Italian cameos, inlay work, and glass mosaic, as well as the styles of the Etruscans, ancient Rome, and the Renaissance.

# Cameo Jewelry

Cameos, a holdover from the empire period that was reinforced by the Victorian enthusiasm for archaeology and Italian culture,

Peter Carl Fabergé (1846–1920) belonged to a French Protestant family that fled France in the 1600s and eventually settled in Russia. He trained as a goldsmith, and besides working in his father's workshop in St. Petersburg, volunteered at the Hermitage Museum, cataloging and repairing the royal jewels. Working with the Russian goldsmith Michael Perchin, he began to replicate the techniques used to make the Hermitage treasures and eventually began to make copies of the objects themselves. He became so good at it that Czar Alexander could not tell which was the original and which was the copy. Fabergé was made supplier to the imperial court as a reward for making the first of the famous Fabergé "surprise" Easter eggs as a gift for the czar's wife Czarina Maria. This first egg, according to Henry Charles Bainbridge in his book *Peter Carl Fabergé*, "was to all appearances an ordinary hen's egg. It was of gold enameled opaque white, and on being opened revealed a yolk also of gold. The yolk opened, and inside was a chicken made in gold of different shades; within the chicken was a model of the Imperial crown, and inside this hung a tiny ruby egg."

*The Surprise Mosaic Egg, created by Peter Carl Fabergé.*

Henry Charles Bainbridge, *Peter Carl Fabergé*. London: Spring Books, 1966, p. 70.

Cameo bracelets such as this one featuring Cupid, Athena, and Mercury were popular during the Victorian age.

continued to be very popular, particularly in parures. Hardstone cameos continued to be carved, and the intaglio also was popular. Subjects for these demanding masterpieces were most often mythological, or at least classical. Such was the demand for cameo jewelry, however, that cameos began to be carved out of the conch shells found in the sea off Naples, which were both plentiful and easier to work than hard stone. While the finest of these shell cameos are also genuine works of art, the vast majority were produced quickly and featured simple subjects that appealed to Victorian sentimentality: birds and flowers, cupids, noncontroversial goddesses like Hebe and Psyche (modestly draped), and most popular of all, the pretty young girl with flowers in her hair and (if the purchaser could afford it) genuine diamond jewelry inset.

Also popular was the "lava" cameo, so named because the carvers traded on the romantic notion that it was made from the lava from Mt. Vesuvius. In fact, lava cameos "are not actually carved in lava, but rather the dark colored limestones that are indigenous to the region around Pompeii . . . the local jewelers and carvers of the 1800s used the romance of Pompeii's volcano and lava flows in an effort to sell their wares."[53] Many lava cameos featured the portrait of a famous artist, poet, or philosopher, such as Leonardo da Vinci, Petrarch, Dante, or Socrates. Bracelets of linked cameos depicting the pantheon of classical gods or the gods of the week (Diana, Mars, Mercury, Jupiter, Venus, Saturn, and Apollo) were also popular.

## *Petra Dura* and Micromosaic

Both Florence and Rome were popular tourist meccas, and few Victorian visitors went home without a sample of either Florentine mosaic (*petra* or *pietra dura*) or Roman mosaic (micromosaic). *Petra dura*, which is still produced today, is not really mosaic but inlay work, which consists of "small pieces of cut stone (often coral, marble, malachite, turquoise, lapis-lazuli and opal), cemented in a pattern into recesses in, usually, a black marble background. The designs were often floral."[54]

In fact, *petra dura* has been made since the Renaissance; the Palazzo Pitti in Florence displays great tables finished with it, depicting mythological scenes surrounded by garlands of fruit and flowers. The loveliest pieces use the natural striations and marbling of the stone to create the effect of shading.

An example of a *petra dura* tabletop; also known as Florentine mosaic.

Micromosaic (miniature mosaic) was a Victorian phenomenon, although something of the sort is still produced under the name of "Italian mosaic." Let the buyer beware: This tourist "jewelry" is crude indeed compared to the delicate work of the 1800s. True Victorian micromosaic is made from tiny bits of glass (tesserae) set into a black glass frame: "Minute subtly coloured *tesserae*, usually cut from thin glass rods, were arranged in mastic or cement on a glass panel using pointed tweezers. When all were in place, the gaps were filled with coloured wax and the surface was polished. Although birds and flowers were popular subjects, the most typical motifs were the buildings and ruins of Rome."[55] The work is sometimes so fine it is hard to distinguish it from painting.

A micromosaic brooch circa 1860. The central medallion is made up of minute glass cubes, or tesserae, of differing shades of colors.

# Classical and Renaissance Revivalism

The Renaissance monuments of Florence, the ruins of Rome, and the archaeological discoveries of the Etruscans and Pompeii combined to inspire an enthusiasm for Italian revivalist styles. Prompted by his artist friend Michelangelo Catena, Fortunato Pio Castellani and after him his sons Alessandro and Augusto pioneered a fashion in "archaeological" jewelry inspired by Etruscan and Pompeian discoveries. The Castellanis also refined the art of micromosaic.

The Castellanis and Carlo Giuliano in Italy and François-Désiré Froment-Meurice, Frédéric-Jules Rudolphi, and Jules Wièse in France promoted a Renaissance revival style that reintroduced the fine modeling and skilled enameling that characterize Renaissance jewelry. So masterful was their workmanship that it is sometimes difficult to tell their Renaissance revival pieces from actual Renaissance jewels.

The long and peaceful Victorian era came to an end with the death of Victoria. The period that followed, known as the Edwardian era, formed a brief transition between the Victorian era and the beginnings of the modern world.

# The Edwardians

The Edwardian era takes its name from England's Edward VII, also known as Bertie or Tum-Tum, England's last merry monarch. It extended from the death of Victoria in 1901 to the outbreak of World War I in 1914. It was mainly characterized not so much by high-society misbehavior, although there was a general relaxing of Victorian stuffiness, as by a growth of politi-

## SENTIMENTAL ODDITY: HAIR JEWELRY

Hair jewelry was the oddest of sentimental oddities of a sentimental age. Originally it was made by loving hands at home, out of one's own hair, the hair of a beloved relation, or best of all, the hair of a beloved dead relation. Normally, hair artfully braided or worked into delicate pictorial effects with seed pearls (for tears) was to be found in brooches and rings, but it was also made into bracelets, and necklaces complete with a locket for a painted miniature or daguerreotype of the dear one. Hair jewelry was particularly well suited to the mourning fashions of the later Victorian era.

Where did all the hair come from to make these articles? Most ladies' dressing tables during the 1800s and early 1900s contained an article known as a hair receiver, a glass or porcelain bowl with a hole in the lid. Into this the lady poked hair plucked from her brush and comb; when the hair receiver was full, the contents were transferred to a cloth bag to be saved for making jewelry and "ratts," pads for puffing up milady's hairdo. Books on the ins and outs of making hair jewelry were popular throughout the 1800s.

cal liberalism, particularly the women's movement and the labor movement. Crinolines and bustles gave way to straight skirts and then to rising hemlines as women marched out into public life. In some circles jewelry kept pace with the trend; in others it was worn by society dames who regarded trends with icy indifference.

# Edwardian Jewelry: Tastes Diverge

Edwardian jewelry split along socioeconomic lines. The upper crust (English aristocracy and American industrialists) favored a frosty echo of the rococo: diamonds and pearls. As silver had been the rococo metal of choice for setting diamonds, so platinum was for the Edwardian elite. Edwardian diamond jewelry has been described as "Lace translated into platinum and diamonds."[56] The strength of platinum made it possible to create very delicate, almost invisible settings, and what little metal did show blended with the whiteness of the stones. "Diamonds and pearls set in platinum were favored for their white-on-white color scheme, and sense of refined elegance and luxury."[57] Alloys of white gold were developed as a cheap substitute for platinum.

High fashion demanded parures built around diamond or pearl choker necklaces that recalled the rococo *esclavage* and cascading diamond and pearl pendant earrings. The late Victorian and the Edwardian taste in diamonds was sustained by the discovery of rich diamond deposits in South Africa.

Sometimes the Edwardian white-on-white was relieved by one or two colored stones. Some subversive ladies combined emeralds and amethysts with their diamonds. The initials for the colors of the stones (green, white, violet), stood for "Give women the vote." The daughters of these would-be New Women turned to the art world to inspire their fashions in jewelry.

# Art Nouveau: The Fluid Fantasy

The young and avant-garde of the Edwardian era favored Art Nouveau over echoes of rococo style. The movement that became known as l'Art Nouveau began in France in the late 1880s and 1890s and in time influenced all the decorative arts. In its jewelry art and fashion merged, and for the first time jewelry came to be thought of as wearable art.

Art Nouveau emphasized the beauties of nature, particularly flower and plant forms, and the sinuous, erotic elegance of the female form. But it also incorporated insects such as grasshoppers and wasps, and other creatures not usually thought of as beautiful. Many pieces reveal a sinister preoccupation with decadence, decay, and death. It is characterized by languorous, fluid curves and a naturalistic lack of formal symmetry. The Art Nouveau movement was strongly influenced by the late 1800s craze for Japanese art.

The greatest of the Art Nouveau artist-jewelers was René Lalique (1860–1945). Like the Russian goldsmith Peter Carl Fabergé, he promoted the idea that a piece of jewelry is a work of art with intrinsic value in its own right, over and above the precious materials it is made of. Lalique did not hesitate to combine precious metals and gems with unconventional materials like horn, rock crystal, and glass to create the effects he wanted.

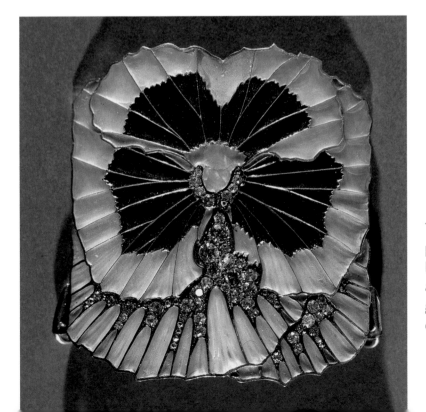

This Art Nouveau plaque created by René Lalique depicts a pansy made of gold, enamel, and diamonds.

# THE TRULY WEIRD: TAXIDERMIC JEWELRY

One of the side effects of extensive Victorian traveling was a fascination with animal life encountered abroad. Often this fascination led to a desire to bring it back dead and wear it, the camera not being a viable alternative in the Victorian world.

That an interest in Egyptian art led to a craze for necklaces made from brightly colored beetles was peculiar enough. Of course the highland practice of making grouse claws into kilt pins had been around for years. But Victorian travelers to foreign climes also adopted an unfortunate habit of bringing back rare creatures to be made into "novelty" jewelry, in something of the same spirit that Edwardian ladies decorated their hats with stuffed birds and nearly wiped out whole species in the process. Among its holdings the British Museum has a necklace made of gold mountings covered with feathers plucked from the heads and breasts of exotic hummingbirds.

He made masterful and original use of enamels. When l'Art Nouveau began to go out of fashion, he turned his attention to glass art, and it is for this that he is best known today.

The changes that rocked the western world between the end of the 1700s and the beginning of the 1800s were nothing compared to the series of cataclysms that brought the comfortable world of the Victorians and Edwardians to an end. In 1914 World War I broke out in Europe. This war, followed by the Russian Revolution, the Great Depression, the atrocities of the Nazis, and the Second World War, ushered in a world that Queen Victoria and King Edward VII could not have imagined. Some of what that world considers jewelry, they would not even recognize.

# The Modern Jeweler's Art

Individualism seems to be the key to modern jewelry design. Jewelers run the gamut from the elegant traditionalism of the Tiffany diamond necklace to eye-catching modern-art-to-wear. There is a great eclecticism to modern jewelry making; that is, the willingness to combine conventional precious materials with highly unconventional ones, precious or otherwise, in highly unconventional ways (what Renaissance goldsmith could have foreseen gutta-percha or Bakelite, acrylic or "found objects" as material for the jeweler's art?). The modern jeweler may draw inspiration from the masterpieces of the past or go off in completely new and unexpected directions. Trends suggest that modern jewelry must above all suit the individual taste of the wearer and the wearer's individual lifestyle. Science is also having an increasing impact on the jeweler's art both in the creation of new materials and techniques and in the refinement of existing ones.

## The Technology of Jewelry Making

One great change in jewelry creation between the present and past centuries is in the technology used to create it. Until the middle of the 1800s the tools and techniques that jewelers used were not very different from those used in ancient Sumer and Egypt. Stone and bronze tools gave way to tools of iron and later steel. Precious stones became more varied and more plentiful. But otherwise, with the exception of the development of refractive diamond cutting and the faceting of colored stones in the 1600s and 1700s, very little had changed. The Industrial Revolution brought machinery for mass-producing gold and silver jewelry and the development of some new materials such as gutta-percha and goldstone. But it was really the great wars and the machine industries of the twentieth century and the technological advances that came out of them that drastically changed how jewelry is made today.

The greatest change to jewelry making in the twentieth and twenty-first centuries is technological precision. Techniques that once depended on the jeweler's eye and sixth sense can now be performed with mechanical precision. For example, where goldsmiths once used kilns fueled with charcoal and regulated with bellows, today they use casting ovens with precision temperature controls. The result is a finer quality of jewelry and a union of art and science that makes the career of a jeweler easier and more satisfying.

Power-assisted tools that combine machine power with the jeweler's skill are also making the jeweler's job easier; for example, the air-powered hammer which the goldsmith uses for doing repoussé or chiseling out channel work. The goldsmith's artistic skill still guides the process, but the machine supplies the force that once had to be provided by human muscle.

# Laser Technology

Laser technology has given jewelers the ability to work directly on pieces of jewelry with more precision than ever before. Laser welding has replaced the jeweler's soldering torches, powered by butane or propane, that had not long before replaced the jeweler's kiln. Laser welding allows such precision in the jeweler's work that, for example, stones need not be removed when jewelry is being repaired, and jewelers can perform tasks that once

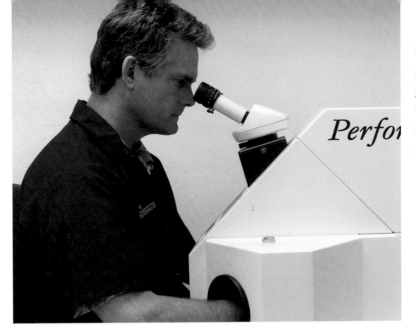

would have been either impossible or too time-consuming to be cost-effective, such as creating special finishing details. Computer-controlled lasers are being used to cut diamonds with greater precision and regularity than can be done by hand.

## Metallurgy and Gemology

Two other areas in which great scientific advances have been made are metallurgy, or the science of refining and working metals, and gemology, the study of precious and semiprecious stones. Advances in metallurgy have produced new alloys that produce superior jewelry. Where once white gold had to be plated with rhodium to make it truly white, new alloys using beryllium, ruthenium, and palladium, intrinsic in the metal, now create a white gold without the need of plating that eventually wears away. The same alloys are being used to make silver that does not tarnish. Metallurgists are working with palladium alone as a jeweler's metal; it has many of the same qualities as platinum and is much less expensive.

A combination of metallurgy and chemistry has resulted in new techniques for electroplating metals; that is, submerging them in a chemical bath and passing an electrical current through them that causes them to become coated with a thin layer of

# A Modern Goldsmith:
## From Hobby to Livelihood

Many people pursue hobbies in their free time. Sometimes a person's hobby can grow from a part-time activity into their full-time profession. This is the case with Gary Lee Chase, a Santa Cruz, California, jeweler. Jewelers are involved in the design, manufacture, repair, appraisal, and sales of all forms of jewelry. Gary got into jewelry making by way of cutting precious stones, which he started to do as a hobby in the early 1970s. In time, he began to sell his gems at craft shows and art fairs, and eventually to jewelry stores. Dissatisfied with the settings other craftsmen made for his stones, he began to experiment with metal working. He built his first bench from two sawhorses and an old door, and began to make silver jewelry with a butane jeweler's torch.

Between 1979 and 1982, Gary studied with the Gemological Institute of America, and earned the title of Graduate Gemologist. He worked for a time for John Sumita, a retail jeweler in San Francisco, before establishing his own trade shop to do repairs, sizing, and custom work for guild-division (high-quality) jewelry stores. He opened his own jewelry store in 1990. His work consists mainly of designing and making custom jewelry.

In an interview with the author, Gary says of his hobby-turned-livelihood, "I love coming in to work every day."

*Jeweler Gary Chase at his work bench.*

another material. Advances in chemistry have made possible attractive new plating techniques such as black rhodium plating. New nontoxic chemical baths have replaced the highly poisonous ones that took such a toll on the workers who used them.

New ways have been developed to artificially produce both high-quality man-created precious stones (stones created by growing crystals in a laboratory under appropriate conditions of heat and pressure) and inexpensive synthetic gemstones (stones manufactured from melted-down minerals that produce a convincing appearance without careful attention to the authenticity of the crystalline structure). Advances have also been made in treating stones with either heat and pressure or diffusion of chemicals into the surface of the stones to enhance or change their color.

## Subatomic Physics

The electron microscope, which uses a beam of electrons instead of visible light to produce images of objects smaller than the wave length of visible light, has had a huge impact on gemologists' understanding of the molecular structure of precious stones. This technology is turning out to be a two-edged sword. On the one hand, it makes it easier for reputable gemologists to identify synthetic and man-created stones and for reputable manufacturers to grow high-quality man-created crystals by increasing their understanding of the crystalline structure of precious stones and the conditions required to recreate it. On the other hand, a deeper understanding of the structure of gemstones makes it easier for unscrupulous dealers to create convincing fakes, like a recent influx of diffusion-treated pink-orange *padparadscha* sapphires from Thailand.

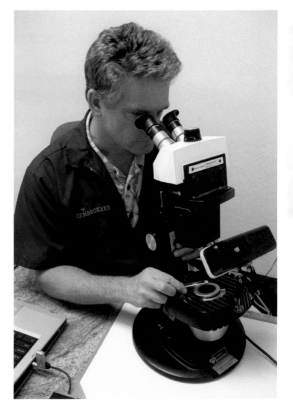

Goldsmith Gary Chase uses a jeweler's microscope to appraise a gemstone.

The color of diamonds can be changed by irradiating them with subatomic particles, then annealing them in a heat-treatment process to alter or intensify their color. This is usually done to turn ordinary white diamonds with less than perfect color into more valuable colored diamonds, although these treated diamonds are not as valuable as the very rare natural colored diamonds. Most blue, green, orange, and pink diamonds used in jewelry today have been treated.

Molecular analysis has initiated some new trends like diamond cutting following the structure of the individual stone instead of adhering to traditional styles of faceted cutting. This is necessary for some specialty stones like black diamonds, which are notoriously idiosyncratic to work with.

## Computer Software

The advent of computer technology made it possible for jewelers to design pieces of jewelry much more easily and also with greater precision. Processes such as CAD/CAM design that once were available only to large corporations because they were enormously expensive, have become affordable to most independent jewelers through the funnel-down effect of new technology. Instead of carving the wax model for lost wax casting directly, goldsmiths today use a CAD/CAM application to design wax carvings electronically, then send the result to a mill that machine-carves the wax model and returns it to the goldsmith for final finishing and texturing by hand. Jewelers also use CAD/CAM to design dies for stamping. The end product is much more detailed than if it had been done by hand and much less expensive to produce in terms of time and labor, a benefit that can be passed along to the customer.

## Twentieth-Century Movements

The two main jewelry movements of the twentieth century, Art Deco and Retro, were strongly influenced by industrial shapes and forms and by the two world wars. The most obvious trends in jewelry making since the middle of the 1900s, however, have been toward an increasing individualism and disregard for the dictates of the fashion industry, and toward rapidly changing styles, with many different ones in effect at the same time. This individualism began with the Studio Art Movement following World War II, and was further influenced by "hippie" counter-culturalism and the women's liberation movement, which encouraged people in general and women in particular to assert themselves and wear whatever they liked and could afford. The trend toward many different, rapidly changing styles is at least partly due to the communication revolution that began with television and exploded in the 1990s with the Internet and the World Wide Web.

## Art Deco (1920 to 1930) and Retro (1935 to 1949)

There is something about war that brings out the assertive in jewelry design. Art Deco came out of the conflagration of

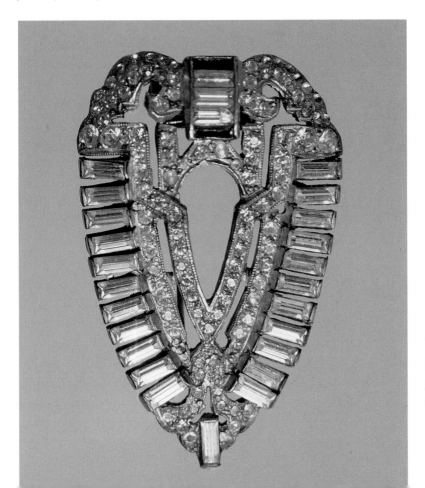

This jewel clip is an example of the geometric Art Deco design.

World War I; Retro was an outgrowth of World War II. Although they are very different in style, both feature big, bold, in-your-face motifs and lots of color.

Art Deco, reacting against the supple curves and subtle colors of Art Nouveau, drew upon geometric and mechanical shapes. French designer Paul Iribe, in 1930, promoted the "sacrifice [of] the flower on the altar of Cubism and the machine."[58] While the movement courted the wealthy with colored stones and black onyx in a pavement of diamonds set in platinum on the old Edwardian model, elsewhere it ran to semiprecious stones like lapis lazuli, amber, and coral, and materials such as glass and Bakelite in large, chunky, boldly colored pieces. The classic Art Deco look is associated with jewelers like Cartier.

Retro was named by François Curiel of Christie's New York in the 1970s, but it was inspired by European designers, many of whom had fled to America, as a finger in the eye of the German aggressor during World War II. "In Paris, the house of Cartier responded to the German defeat of France in apt fashion. It showed its unbowed spirit by creating its fanciful animalier style. Animal figures in gold, studded with gems and enhanced by shining enamel, reaffirmed the power of joy and beauty in the face of the Nazi occupation."[59]

Since platinum was co-opted by the war effort, retro pieces are mostly of gold and rose gold—large, flamboyant three-dimensional pieces set with aquamarine, amethyst, citrine, topaz, and synthetic colored gems. It favored explosive loops, floral sprays, and bows suggesting Fourth-of-July fireworks, as well as the animalier style.

# The Studio Jewelry Movement (1940 to Present)

The idea of jewelry as wearable art, introduced by Lalique, is still in force. In fact, much of what is called art jewelry is art first and only incidentally wearable. Art jewelry began with the Studio Art Movement, which was started as rehabilitation therapy for World War II veterans and branched out into as many different

"The Dancer," a brooch designed by American studio jeweler Ed Wiener circa 1947, is a well-known example of mid-twentieth century studio jewelry.

styles and directions as there were designers. The Studio Art Movement underlies the strong individuality of fashions in jewelry today.

Studio art jewelry did follow certain trends. Design analyst Susan Grant Lewin says of the movement, "The leitmotif that bound all of these studio jewelers together was the desire to apply the then current tenets of modernism, such as biomorphism, primitivism, and constructivism to jewelry."[60] Biomorphism follows organic shapes, including microorganisms; primitivism is inspired by the folk art of so-called primitive people; constructivism incorporates architectural forms and geometric shapes.

The Studio Art Movement also carried the Art Nouveau disregard for precious materials to the ultimate extreme,

Antipreciousism. In combination with precious metals and precious and semiprecious stones, jewelry was made out of base metals such as copper, iron, steel, and aluminum; hardware such as plumbing supplies, paper clips, typewriter keys; and most recently and effectively, computer components; plastics, wood, stones, beads and buttons, textiles and leather, newspaper clippings, papier mâché, and found objects.

The Pop and Funk spin-offs from the Studio Art Movement contributed social commentary and shock effect. Says Lewin, "This was jewelry intended to shock, and it did. Ken Cory . . . employed organic, sensual forms of cast plastic or leather with copper, stones, often narrative enamelwork, and found objects."[61] The "narrative enamelwork" was often obscene or political in nature, and the design of the jewelry was often explicitly sexual or political.

Studio jewelry artists explored surface effects such as three-dimensional constructions, texture, and the application of textile arts such as knitting and crocheting to metal. Special color effects were achieved with the use of precious and semiprecious stones, with emphasis not on their value but on the way their colors and textures interacted. New styles and materials in enameling were explored, as were combinations of precious and base metals, and new metals such as "titanium, tantalum, and niobium, all of which change color when exposed to specific electric currents while immersed in an electrolytic solution."[62] Raw crystals of precious and semiprecious stones were incorporated for their unusual color and textural effects.

Some of this "wearable art" was wearable only if the wearer was a professional model who knew how to move very, very carefully. Lewin says of one artist-jeweler that he "viewed the body as an armature [support] for the work, an extraordinary and unprecedented concept for his day."[63]

Lewin sums up modern art jewelry by saying, "All in all, we have come full circle from the nascence of what some now call American art jewelry. . . . American jewelry had never been so rich in technical expertise, material diversity, formal innovation, and sheer energy."[64]

# A Spirit of Adventure

Barbara Cartlidge, author of *Twentieth-Century Jewelry*, has this to say of fashions in jewelry from 1970 onward:

> By the early 1970s, the last vestiges of etiquette in clothing and jewellery had really disappeared: "anything goes." Although there were still social groups, it was hard to distinguish them by their jewellery. For some people, it will always be important to have very expensive, precious jewelry, but this is now a matter of personal choice (and being able to afford it) rather than a social "must."[65]

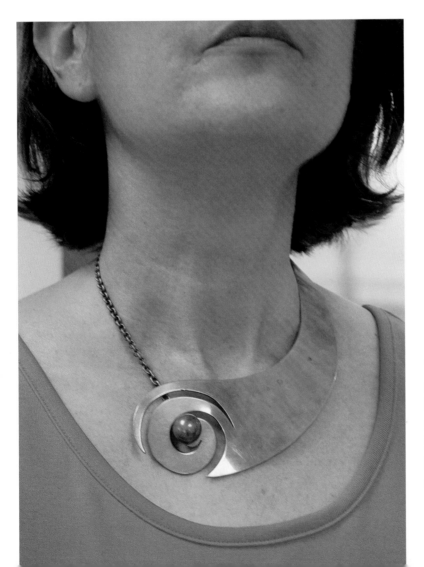

This unique brass collar, designed by famed American studio jeweler Art Smith in the 1950s, is a prime example of "wearable art."

In other words, the spirit imbuing modern jewelers and jewelry wearers is not very different from that of the Renaissance in its delight in exploration and imagination and particularly in its strong emphasis on individualism, both in the artist-jeweler and in the wearer.

Although there have been many reasons for wearing jewelry down through the centuries—social and political prestige, religious or magical significance, sentiment—the principal reason for wearing jewelry today is enjoyment. Whether a person buys it from a jeweler, makes it, or works with a goldsmith to select materials and design pieces, jewelry is above all an expression of personal taste, and wearing it should be a joyous experience.

# Notes

## Chapter 1: Ancient Times (to 500 B.C.)

1. Quoted in P.R.S. Moorey, *"Ur of the Chaldees": A Revised and Updated Edition of Sir Leonard Woolley's Excavations at Ur.* Ithaca, NY: Cornell University Press, 1982, pp. 58–59.
2. Quoted in Moorey, *"Ur of the Chaldees,"* p. 67.
3. Quoted in I.E.S. Edwards, *The Treasures of Tutankhamun.* New York: Viking, 1972, p. 34.
4. Hans Wolfgang Müller and Eberhard Thiem, *Gold of the Pharaohs.* Ithaca, NY: Cornell University Press, 1999, p. 30.
5. Müller and Thiem, *Gold of the Pharaohs,* p. 32.
6. Müller and Thiem, *Gold of the Pharaohs,* p. 29.
7. Müller and Thiem, *Gold of the Pharaohs,* p. 25.

## Chapter 2: The Greeks and the Romans (500 B.C. to A.D. 500)

8. Quoted in Hellenic Silver- and Goldsmith Centre, *Greek Jewelry: 5000 Years of Tradition.* www.add.gr/jewel/elka/ index.html.
9. Guido Gregorietti, *Jewelry Through the Ages.* New York: American Heritage, 1969, p. 64.
10. Quoted in Hellenic Silver- and Goldsmith Centre, *Greek Jewelry.*
11. Quoted in Hellenic Silver- and Goldsmith Centre, *Greek Jewelry.*
12. Gregorietti, *Jewelry Through the Ages,* p. 30.
13. Pliny (Gaius Plinius Secundus) the Elder, *Loeb Classical Library: Natural History,* IX.58, trans. H. Rackham. Cambridge, MA: Harvard University Press, 1983.
14. Pliny, *Natural History,* XXXVII.4.
15. Pliny, *Natural History,* XXXVII.76.
16. Associated Press, "Field Museum Exhibit Focuses on Death in Pompeii," October 22, 2005. http://cbs2chicago.com/topstories/local_story_295141843.html.
17. John Ward-Perkins and Amanda Claridge, *Pompeii, A.D. 79.* New York: Alfred A. Knopf, 1978, p. 135.

## Chapter 3: The Early Middle Ages (A.D. 500 to 1000)

18. Quoted in Hellenic Silver- and Goldsmith Centre, *Greek Jewelry.*
19. Quoted in Hellenic Silver- and Goldsmith Centre, *Greek Jewelry.*
20. Robert Browning, *Justinian and Theodora.* New York: Praeger, 1971, p. 69.
21. Shaquilat Sergius, "Iconography of San Vitale," Ancient Worlds: Byzantium.

www.ancientworlds.net/aw/Post/350801.

22. Sergius, "Iconography of San Vitale."
23. Quoted in Roman Finds Group, "New Finds, Autumn 2003." www.romanfindsgroup.org.uk/finds.html.
24. Gregorietti, *Jewelry Through the Ages*, p. 139.
25. Gregorietti, *Jewelry Through the Ages*, p. 139.
26. Jeff Clarke, "Viking Ornamentation Styles." http://mahan.wonkwang.ac.kr/link/med/viking/vikorn.htm.

Chapter 4: The Romanesque and Gothic Eras (A.D. 1000 to 1450)

27. Gregorietti, *Jewelry Through the Ages*, p. 149.
28. Gregorietti, *Jewelry Through the Ages*, p. 149.
29. Gregorietti, *Jewelry Through the Ages*, p. 150.
30. Gregorietti, *Jewelry Through the Ages*, p. 150.
31. Gregorietti, *Jewelry Through the Ages*, p. 154.
32. Joan Evans, *A History of Jewelry: 1100–1870*. Boston: Boston Book and Art, 1970, p. 53.
33. Evans, *A History of Jewelry*, p. 55.

Chapter 5: The Renaissance (A.D. 1450 to 1600)

34. Daniela Mascetti and Amanda Triossi, *The Necklace: From Antiquity to the Present*. New York: Harry N. Abrams, 1997, p. 53.
35. Evans, *A History of Jewelry*, p. 81.
36. Gregorietti, *Jewelry Through the Ages*, p. 190.
37. Gregorietti, *Jewelry Through the Ages*, pp. 190–92.

38. Central European University, "Medieval Jewelry." www.ceu.hu/medstud/manual/SRM/jewel.htm.
39. Evans, *A History of Jewelry*, p. 83.
40. *Vogue Gioiello*, "The Jewelry of Madonnas and Queens." www.voguegioiello.net/06per/perle/01sto/0505/eindex.asp.

Chapter 6: Baroque and Rococo (A.D. 1600 to 1815)

41. Gregorietti, *Jewelry Through the Ages*, p. 212.
42. Mascetti and Triossi, *The Necklace*, p. 59.
43. Mascetti and Triossi, *The Necklace*, p. 59.
44. Mascetti and Triossi, *The Necklace*, p. 63.
45. Mascetti and Triossi, *The Necklace*, p. 61.
46. Gregorietti, *Jewelry Through the Ages*, p. 239.
47. Gregorietti, *Jewelry Through the Ages*, p. 237.

Chapter 7: The Victorians and Edwardians (A.D. 1815 to 1915)

48. Ginny Redington Dawes and Corinne Davidov, *Victorian Jewelry: Unexplored Treasures*. New York: Abbeville, 1991, p. 90.
49. Mascetti and Triossi, *The Necklace*, p. 87.
50. Roy B. Chamberlin and Herman Feldman, eds., *Dartmouth Bible*, 2nd ed. Boston: Houghton Mifflin, 1961, p. 76.
51. Dawes and Davidov, *Victorian Jewelry*, p. 124.
52. Claire Phillips, *Jewels and Jewelry: 500 Years of Western Jewelry from the World-Renowned Collection of the*

*Victoria and Albert Museum*. New York: Watson-Guptill, 2000, p. 74.

53. The Jewelry Experts, Bijoux Extraordinaire, Ltd., "Victorian Lava Cameos." www.jewelryexpert.com/catalog/cameo4.htm.

54. Anita Mason and Dianne Packer, *An Illustrated Dictionary of Jewelry*. New York: Harper & Row, 1974, p. 250.

55. Phillips, *Jewels and Jewelry*, p. 74.

56. R.F. Moeller Jeweler, "Edwardian Jewelry." www.rfmoeller.com/estate/edwardia.htm.

57. Antique Jewelry Online, "Edwardian Jewelry." www.antiquejewelryonline.com/learn/edwardian.htm.

## Chapter 8: The Modern Jeweler's Art

58. Quoted in Phillips, *Jewels and Jewelry*, p. 112.

59. Mondera, "Retro 1940–1949." www.mondera.com/learn/retro.asp?nmcssid=classid%3D111.

60. Susan Grant Lewin, *One of a Kind: American Art Jewelry Today*. New York: Harry N. Abrams, 1994, p. 34.

61. Lewin, *One of a Kind*, p. 40.

62. Lewin, *One of a Kind*, p. 53.

63. Lewin, *One of a Kind*, p. 35.

64. Lewin, *One of a Kind*, p. 56.

65. Quoted in Phillips, *Jewels and Jewelry*, p. 124.

**alloy:** A mixture or amalgam of two or more metals.

**Antipreciousism:** A movement that promotes the use of nonprecious materials in the making of jewelry.

**Art Nouveau:** A movement in the decorative arts in the late 1800s and early 1900s, featuring undulating, flowing curves, an emphasis on natural forms, and in jewelry, the use of unconventional materials such as horn, ivory, and glass.

**brooch:** A large decorative pin or clasp.

**Byzantium:** The Eastern Roman Empire with its seat at Constantinople.

**cameo:** A relief carving in stone against a flat background, particularly one in which the color of the carving contrasts with the background.

**casting:** Pouring molten metal into a mold in which it solidifies.

**classical:** Of Greek history, pertaining to the period between 500 and 400 B.C. Of art and culture, pertaining to the Greeks and the Romans.

**diadem:** A crown or ornamental headdress.

**die:** A tool used for molding or stamping designs in metal.

**engrave:** To hammer or carve a design into a surface.

**Funk:** An art movement of the 1960s that used unconventional materials, often found objects, to create visually shocking images with social relevance.

**iconography:** A set of traditional symbolic forms and figures associated with a subject, particularly Christianity.

**man-created stone:** A man-made precious stone grown from a crystal under the proper conditions of heat and pressure. Its molecular and crystalline structure is identical to those of its natural equivalent.

**metallurgy:** The science of refining and working metals and understanding their properties.

**naturalism:** The practice of depicting subjects as realistically as possible in the visual arts.

**neoclassical:** A style of jewelry derived from classical Greece and Rome, featuring simple lines, gold work, and opaque or cabochon stones and cameos.

**parure:** A matched set of jewelry consisting of a necklace, earrings, bracelets, one or more brooches, and possibly rings, hair ornaments, and buckles. A demi-parure ("half-parure") is a set of two or three matching pieces.

**Pop:** An art movement in the early 1960s that used images from everyday life to comment on the banality of society.

**revivalist style:** A style imitating the style or styles of an earlier time.

**semiprecious stone:** Any gemstone other than the diamond, emerald, ruby, sapphire, or precious amethyst.

**zoomorphic:** Animal-shaped, or having animal-shaped elements.

# For Further Reading

## Books

Ginny Redington Dawes and Corinne Davidov, *Victorian Jewelry: Unexplored Treasures*. New York: Abbeville Press Publishers, 1991. Lavishly illustrated volume on the lesser-known aspects of Victorian jewelry. The sections on agate jewelry and hair jewelry are especially good.

Katharine Stoddard Gilbert, ed., *Treasures of Tutankhamun*. New York: Ballantine, 1976. Beautifully illustrated catalog that accompanied the 1979 traveling exhibit.

Ellen D. Reeder, ed., *Scythian Gold: Treasures from Ancient Ukraine*. New York: Harry N. Abrams, 1999. Lavishly illustrated catalog that accompanied the 1999–2001 traveling exhibit.

Marbeth Schon, *Modernist Jewelry 1930–1960: The Wearable Art Movement*. Atglen, PA: Schiffer Books, 2004. A well-written exploration of the work of 175 of the most important American studio jewelers through four pivotal exhibitions held at the Museum of Modern Art (1946) and The Walker Art Center in Minneapolis (1948, 1955, 1959).

John Ward-Perkins and Amanda Claridge, *Pompeii, A.D. 79*. New York: Alfred A. Knopf, 1978. Intelligently written and beautifully illustrated catalog that accompanied the 1979 traveling exhibit.

Michael Wood, *In Search of the Dark Ages*. New York: Facts On File, 1987. Scholarly and well-written discussion of several early medieval figures and archaeological finds, with informative illustrations. Especially good on the Sutton Hoo ship burial.

## Periodicals

Rick Gore, "After 2000 Years of Silence, the Dead Do Tell Tales at Vesuvius," *National Geographic*, May, 1984. Fascinating article about Sara Bisel's forensic reconstructions of the dead of Herculaneum.

## Web Sites

**American Museum of Natural History** (www.amnh.org). Good overview of the history of diamonds in jewelry.

**Art of the First Cities: The Third Millennium B.C. from the Mediterranean to the Indus** (www.metmuseum.org/ex plore/First_Cities/firstcities_main. htm). A beautifully designed and detailed site by the Metropolitan Museum of Art that covers the earliest cities from the Aegean to the Indus Valley.

The section on Sumeria and Ur is especially good. The zoom-in feature on works of art is especially helpful.

**The British Museum Compass Collections Online** (www.thebritishmuseum.ac.uk/compass/ixbin/hixclient.exe?_IXDB_=compass&search-form=graphical/main.html&submit-button=search). A wealth of information about the treasures of the British Museum, easily searchable.

**Greek Jewelry: 5000 Years of Tradition** (www.add.gr/jewel/elka/index.html).

Very thoroughly illustrated overview of Greek jewelry from prehistory to the present day, complete with diagrams of jewelry-making tools and techniques.

**Medieval Jewelry** (www.ceu.hu/med-stud/manual/SRM/jewel.htm). Part of the Web site of the Department of Medieval Studies of Central European University. A scholarly and readable source on medieval jewelry, its wearers, and the artists who made it.

# Index

Aigrette, *71*, 72
Albert (prince of Saxe-
  Coburg-Gotha), 77, 78,
  *79*, 80
Alloys
  advances in metallurgy
    and, 91
  in goldwork, 12, 26
Antipreciousism, 98
Apollonides, 28
Art Deco, 94, *95*, 95–96
Art Nouveau, 86–87, *87*

Bainbridge, Henry
  Charles, 81
Band necklaces, 70–71
Baroque era, 63, 64–67
Beadwork
  Egyptian, 17–18
  Greek/Roman, 26
  Sumerian, *11*, 13
Belts, jeweled, of Gothic
  era, 51
Blanche of Lancaster, 53
Bonaparte, Napoléon, 75
Boticelli, 56
Bracelets, cameo, *82*
Brooches
  Byzantine, *41*
  of early Middle Ages,
    39–40
  Gothic, *49*, 50–51, 51
  of Renaissance, 60–62
  rococo, 67, 69–70
  Romanesque, 45
  of Studio Art

Movement, *97*
Byzantine empire
  influences on jeweler's art
    of, 33–34
  jewelry of, *33, 34, 35*

Cabochons, 18, 26
Cameos, 28
  Gothic, 49–50
  origin of, 28
  of Renaissance, 59, 61
  Victorian, 80, 81, *82*, 82
Canning Jewel, 61–62
Carnavon, George
  Herbert, Lord, 15
Carter, Howard, 15, 18
Cartier, 96
Castellani family, 84
Casting, 24
Cartlidge, Barbara, 99
Cellini, Benvenuto, 58
Celtic knot, 41
Chase, Gary Lee, *92*, 92,
  *93*
Cloisonné, 17
Columbus, Christopher, 55
Computer software, 94
Costanza of Aragon
  (Spanish queen), 47–48
  crown of, *48*
Cronius, 28
Croom, Alex, 39
Crowns
  of Costanza of Aragon,
    *48*
  *See also* Diadems

Curiel, François, 96

Diadems (crowns), *15*
  Greek, 22–23
  of Queen Puabi, 13–15
  Romanesque, 52–53
Diamonds
  baroque developments in
    cutting, 64–65
  changing color of, 94
  in Edwardian jewelry, 86
  of Gothic era, 49
  refractive cutting of, 90
  of rococo era, 67, 69
Dioscurides, 28
Du Barry, Madame, 72

Earrings
  Byzantine, *36*
  of Gothic era, 51–52
  Hellenistic, *23*
  of Renaissance, 57
Edward VIII (English
  king), 84
Edwardian era, 85–86
Egypt, 16–19
Electroplating, 91, 93
Elizabeth I (English
  queen), *57*
Empire period, jewelry
  styles of, 75
Enamelwork
  Egyptian, 17
  Greek, 26
  narrative, 98
  Renaissance techniques

in, 58–59
*Englishwoman's Domestic Magazine*, 77
Etruscans, 27

Fabergé, Peter Carl, 81
Faience, 17
Feudalism, 45
Florentine Rooster, 62
Founder's Jewel, 51

Gemstones
baroque, 64–65
in Byzantine jewelry, 36
in Edwardian jewelry, 86
molecular analysis of, 93–94
Renaissance techniques in, 59
in rococo era, 65
synthetic, 93
*Girl with a Pearl Earring* (Vanmeer), *66*
Giuliano, Carlo, 84
Gold
from the Americas, 55
Greek use of, 24–26
qualities of, 12
Golden Helmet of Mescalamdug, 12–13
Goldsmiths
Egyptian, 17
first distinction between jewelers and, 49
of Gothic era, 52
modern technology and, 90, 91, 93
of Renaissance, 60
of Romanesque era, 46
Gonzaga Cameo, 28
Gothic era, 48–53
Greece, Ancient
jewelry making of, 21–22
metalworking of, 22–26
Gutta-percha, 80

Hair, Renaissance style of, 55
Hair jewelry, 85
Henry IV (English king), 52
Henry VIII (English king), 56–57
Herculaneum, 80
Holbein, Hans, 56, 57–58
Hope, Henry Phillip, 68
Hope Diamond, 68, *68*, 74

Industrial Revolution, 75, 76, 90
Inlay work, Egyptian, 19
Intaglio, 26, 28
Iribe, Paul, 96
Isabelle de Valois (French princess), 52, 53

Jellinge style, 41–43
John the Fearless (Duke of Burgundy), 50
Justinian (Byzantine emperor), 38

Lalique, René, 87
Language of Flowers, 78
Lapis lazuli, 13, 80
Laser technology, 90–91, *91*
Lollia Paulina, 26
Lost wax method, 24
Louis XIV (French king), 68
Louis XV (French king), 72
Louis XVI (French king), 68, 73
Lovers Brooch, 51

Marie Antoinette, 63, *73*
necklace of, 72–73
Mazarin cut, 64
Metalwork
Greek, *24*
of Hellenistic period, 22–26

Micromosaic, 83–84
Middle Ages, early, 32, 38–39
jewelry making in, 39–42
Sutton Hoo treasure, 42–43
*See also* Byzantine empire
Modern jewelry
materials of, 89
technology and, 90–91 93–94
Molecular analysis, 93–94
Mosaics
Byzantine, 36
Florentine, *83*
micromosaics, 83–84
Motifs
Art Deco, 96
Byzantine, 34, 35
of early Middle Ages, 39, 42
Greek, 23
rococo, 69–70
Victorian, 77–78
Mourning jewelry, 78–79

Necklaces
Art Deco, *95*
of Gothic era, 51–52
of Marie Antoinette, 72–74
pearl, *65*, 66
rococo, 71–73
Niello, 35–36, 43
in Anglo Saxon jewelry, 40
Noah Cameo, 50

Opus interassile, 35, 36

Palladium, 91
Pallavicino, Barbara, 56
Parures, 30, 56
rococo, 70–72
Victorian, 80
Patti, Adelina, 79
Pearls

in baroque jewelry, 60, 66
in Byzantine jewelry, 36
Penannular brooch, 40
Pendants, Renaissance-era, *60*
Perchin, Michael, 81
Peruzzi cut, 64
*Peter Carl Fabergé* (Bainbridge), 81
Petra dura, *83*, 83
Platinum, 91, 99
Pliny the Elder, 26, 28
Poison rings, 57
Pompeii, 80
  emerald necklace of, 29–30
  excavations of, 28–29
  jewelry of, *30*
Portrait lockets, 79
Puabi (queen of Ur), 10, 15
  diadem of, 13–15
Pyrgoteles, 28

Raedwald (king of East Angles), 43
Religious jewelry
  Byzantine, 35
  of Romanesque era, 46
Renaissance (1450-1600), 53
  influences on jewelry of, 55
  jeweler's techniques in, 58–59
Repoussé, 25
Retro, 95–96
Ribbon bows, 66–67, *67*
Richard II (English king), 52, 53
Rings
  Byzantine, *35*
  of renaissance, 57
  wedding, 78
Riviére, 71–72
Rococo era, 63–64
  diamonds in, 69
  necklace styles of, 70–72
Romanesque era, 44–45
  jewelry making of, 44–47
Romans
  characteristics of jewelry of, 31
  stonework of, 26, 28
Rudolphi, Frédéric-Jules, 84

Scythians, 29
Self-adornment, 8
Seymour, Jane, 56
Signet rings, 57
Stasinopoulos, Elizabeth, 21–22, 23, 24–25, 35–36
Stonework, 13
  of Ancient Greece, 28
  Egyptian, 18
  Sumerian, *11*
Studio Art Movement, 95, 96–98, *97, 99*
Subatomic physics, 91–92
Sumer, 11–15
Surprise Mosaic Egg (Fabergé), *81*
Sutton Hoo treasure, 42–43
Tavernier, Jean-Baptiste de, 65, 66, 74
Taxidermic jewelry, 88

Technology, in modern jewelry making, 89–91, 93–94
Theodora (Byzantine empress), 36–38, *37*
Tomb of Gold at Canosa, 26
Toutin, Jean, 67
Tovsta Mohyla pectoral, 29
Tutankhamen (Egyptian pharaoh), 15, 18
  burial mask of, *19*, 19–20
*Twentieth Century Jewelry* (Cartlidge), 99

Vermeer, Jan, 66
Vespucci, Simonetta, 56
Victoria (English queen), 76, 77, *78, 79*
Victorian era
  classical/Renaissance revivalism in, 82, 83, 84–85
  middle-class jewelry of, 80
  mourning jewelry of, 78–79
  taxidermic jewelry of, 88

Wearable art, 87, 96, *99*
Wiener, Ed, *97*
Wièse, Jules, 84
Winston, Harry, 68
Woolley, Charles Leonard, 11, 12–13, 13–14
World War I, 88, 96
World War II, 88, 96
Wykeham, William of, 51

# Picture Credits

Cover: © Araldo de Luca/Corbis

© Adam Woolfitt/CORBIS, 27
© Archivo Iconografico, S.A./CORBIS, 37, 55
The Art Archive/Archeological Museum Naples/Dagli Orti, 24, 30
The Art Archive/Dagli Orti, 70, 95
The Art Archive/Private Collection/Dagli Orti; © 2007 Artists Rights Society (ARS), New York/ADAGP, Paris, 87
The Art Archive/Topkapi Museum Istanbul/Dagli Orti, 71
Arte & Immagini srl/CORBIS, 9, 36
© Bettmann/CORBIS, 57
The British Museum/HIP/The Image Works, 11, 49, 51, 60, 77, 82
© Christie's Images/CORBIS, 23
© Colin Anderson/CORBIS, 65
© Eliol Ciol/CORBIS, 82
© Francis G. Mayer/CORBIS, 66

© Historical Picture Archive/CORBIS, 67
© Jonathan Blair/CORBIS, 41
Mansell/Time Life Pictures/Getty Images, 28, 73
© Mary Evans Picture Library/The Image Works, 15
© Museum of London/HIP/The Image Works, 79
© Peter Harholdt/CORBIS, 83
Photo by Don Barsell, 91, 92, 93
Photo by Marbeth Schon; collection of Jill Crawford, 99
Photo by Shirley Byrne; collection of Marbeth Schon, 97
© Roger Wood/CORBIS, 19
© Seat Archive/Alinari Archives/The Image Works, 48
© Smithsonian Institution/CORBIS, 68
© Tim Graham/CORBIS, 81
© Werner Forman/CORBIS, 33, 34, 35

# About the Author

Katherine Macfarlane grew up in the Great Southwest Desert and became a rock hound and fossil hunter almost as soon as she could toddle. One of her happiest memories is of going to dig trilobites and fossil fish with her father, carrying her very own geologist's hammer. Her interest in jewelry was kindled by the beautiful Navajo and Zuni silver work she collected on vacations to the Grand Canyon.

Another of Katherine's great loves is language. She started reading spontaneously at about age three, and she has not stopped yet. She studied Spanish as a child and Italian as an undergraduate. She has a master's degree in English philology (history of the English language) and a PhD in classics (Greek and Latin studies). Katherine has been a writer all her life; most recently, a technical writer for computer software.

Katherine is also deeply interested in history and archaeology, with excursions into historical anthropology and paleontology. For relaxation, Katherine draws, paints, designs jewelry, and watches birds with her four above-average cats.